Without Pretense

The Final Resolution Of The Multiple Wife Controversy

*A Wholistic Guide For Establishing,
Correcting and Maintaining Perfect
Male/Female Relationships*

Dr. Haraymiel Ben Shaleahk

*Global Images International Press
& Trafford Publishing Ltd.*

A cataloguing record for this book that includes the U.S. Library of Congress Classification number, the Library of Congress Call number and the Dewey Decimal cataloguing code is available from the National Library of Canada. The complete cataloguing record can be obtained from the National Library's online database at: www.nlc-bnc.ca/amicus/index-e.html
ISBN: 1-4120-1722-X

TRAFFORD

This book was published *on-demand* in cooperation with Trafford Publishing. On-demand publishing is a unique process and service of making a book available for retail sale to the public taking advantage of on-demand manufacturing and Internet marketing. **On-demand publishing** includes promotions, retail sales, manufacturing, order fulfilment, accounting and collecting royalties on behalf of the author.

Suite 6E, 2333 Government St., Victoria, B.C. V8T 4P4, CANADA

Phone	250-383-6864	Toll-free	1-888-232-4444 (Canada & US)
Fax	250-383-6804	E-mail	sales@trafford.com
Web site	www.trafford.com	TRAFFORD PUBLISHING IS A DIVISION OF TRAFFORD HOLDINGS LTD.
Trafford Catalogue #03-2099		www.trafford.com/robots/03-2099.html

10   9   8   7   6   5   4   3   2

TABLE OF CONTENTS

Acknowledgements

I want to thank the Hebrew Israelite Community's Ministry of Divine Information in Washington, D.C. and its main branch in Dimona, Israel for providing vital research information needed in this book. I want to further extend my special thanks to my wives for their unwavering support and assistance, without which this work would not have been possible.

To my wife of ten years, Gheliyah, who worked side-by-side with me from the moment I set a schedule for completion and began working in earnest towards that liveline, I offer my profound gratitude, thanks and appreciation. It was her editing skills and many hours of typing the quotations, statistical data and scriptural references used, that contributed much to the finished product and its completion in a reasonable period of time.

Additionally, I thank Gheliyah for writing the Foreword and back cover of this book. By walking step by step with me through the process of writing this book, she has gained tremendous insight and understanding of what I was attempting to achieve through this writing. To Nasiyah, my wife of thirty nine years, who put up with Gheliyah's and my constant absence (often times mine, even when I was physically present) as we endeavored to bring this work to completion. I offer my eternal love, gratitude and appreciation for helping to make this book possible.

It was her back up and support of both Gheliyah and me, covering all the bases we left uncovered, that allowed us the time to focus relatively undisturbed, on this project. Also, my thanks to Nasiyah for writing the "About the Author" section of this book. Having been my life long companion, wife, friend and confidant, she knows me better than most. After all, I have spent more time with her than I have with anyone else on the planet.

My thanks also goes to my dear and special friend of many years, Sister Yahlee, who added her invaluable English language expertise to the editing of this book. (Since the first printing she has become my wife). I give my special thanks to Brother Shavaht and his wife Sister Roneet, for providing the perfect solitary refuge I needed to complete the first draft of this work.

Finally, I want to express my appreciation for some special brothers and sisters who have acted as sounding boards and unofficial consultants on this project: Brothers Ameshadye, Amishoov, Avimelik and Horaliel, your willingness to discuss this subject and provide positive male perspectives proved to be invaluable. Likewise, long discussions with Sisters Elyeefah, Shalamiyah, Adina E. Moniel, Aturah Yoahnah (Dr. Yo) and Kilkeeyah gave me that special feminine perspective I needed to keep things properly balanced.

I also thank all those who I have been involved in counseling. The sessions with you have helped me to gain the much-needed experience and insight required to make this project a viable possibility.

Note To Our Readers

Some of the information in this book has been gathered from actual case histories. These have been carefully selected because of their ability to graphically illustrate particular points being discussed. In some instances where such case histories are used, names and detailed personal information have been changed to protect the privacy of the persons involved. In other instances, the actual names have been used with the permission of the persons involved.

Scriptural references are provided throughout to assist the reader in understanding the "authority source" on which various points are based. Each biblical reference is *written in italics* for easy recognition, and each is an exact quotation from the Scofield Reference Bible. The only exceptions are in cases where New World translations may require us to substitute a word. Whenever this occurs, the substituted word will appear *(in parenthesis)* while the rest of the quotation will remain unchanged.

You will notice that certain word combinations such as Divine Marriage, Divine Pursuit, Divine Relationship and Divine Mecodeshet appear in capitalized form. We are well aware that this usage may not conform to the generally-accepted norms of the English language. You will likewise notice that certain individual words or phrases like Yah, Divine, Sons or Daughters of Yah and Saints will also appear in capitalized form. When they appear in such formal usage, it denotes their application as a principle "building block" or concept in the New World Order.

Also included, is a glossary of terms and phrases used, that may be unfamiliar to some readers. However, the definition of some terms used are so important to your understanding that they are being included at this early point:

Yah- The Creator; the higher spiritual force representing righteousness, love, peace and all things positive and good.

Kingdom of Yah- A New World Order governed by men that are governed by Yah; a society set in order by men set in order by Yah; containing homes established by the Yah-family wherein children honor their father and mother, woman respects her man and man is in the image of Yah.

Divine Marriage- The culmination of the courtship and marriage process within the Hebrew Community; the Holy Institution designed by Yah to form Divine unions between men and women for the perpetuation of His Divine Cycles throughout the creation.

Divine Mecodeshet- The stage of the courtship process prior to Divine Marriage within the Hebrew Israelite marital system; the point of the relationship wherein the community and the priesthood become officially involved.

Divine Pursuit- One of the early informal stages of the developing relationship between a man and a woman according to the guidelines and principles of Yah; an initial part of the courtship process within the Hebrew Israelite Community of Jerusalem; akin to "dating" but much more structured and Yah-oriented.

Divine Relationship- The proper interaction between men and women according to the guidelines of Yah.

Dedication

This book is dedicated to the memory of my youngest daughter *Heterah*, who passed from this plane of existence at the age of sixteen, just prior to the completion of these writings. As her father, I had looked forward to us having a long life together wherein I would be able to teach her of the things you are about to read. It is my heart-felt belief that had she had the opportunity to learn, and the wisdom to employ the teachings in this book, she would have been assured a joyously Holy and Divine Relationship and Marriage. It is also dedicated to my other daughters Ahaviah, Neiyah, Georgia and Roeeyah.

This book is also dedicated to the African Hebrew Israelites, an outstanding community of former African Americans and others of diverse ethnic backgrounds, headquartered in Dimona, Israel. They have taken on the challenge of becoming the vanguard to usher in the prophetic Kingdom of Yah. A kingdom wherein the laws, statutes and commandments of Yah are national policy and govern every aspect of the lives of the people.

This prophetic messianic Kingdom, spoken of in the Holy Scriptures, was to be established in the last days to bring peace, joy and the love of Yah to the whole creation. The Kingdom of Yah can be best understood when simply and properly defined as "a government of men and women governed by Yah." By taking this valiant stand, they have opened up the way to a brighter tomorrow for all humanity, for these are truly – **"The Last Days"**.

> In 1967, at the zenith of the Black revolt in America, approximately 350 men, women and children left the confines of the United States

13

enroute to Israel, via Liberia West Africa. After a successful sojourn of two-and-one half years in the interior of Liberia, where a myriad of negative and unbecoming traits were purged, the remnant of these pioneers moved on to Israel in 1969. Since that time, Ben Ammi and his followers have struggled to establish the long-awaited Kingdom of Yah – on earth!

God the Black Man and Truth
by Ben Ammi, Communicators Press

"And in the days of these kings shall the (Yah) of heaven set up a kingdom, which shall never be destroyed; and the kingdom shall not be left to other people, but it shall break in pieces and consume all these kingdoms, and it shall stand forever."

Daniel 2:44

This work is likewise dedicated to His Excellency Prince Asiel Ben Israel, International Ambassador Plentipotentiary of the Hebrew Israelites of Jerusalem. He has been a constant motivation and source of Divine Inspiration in my quest for Yah. His unselfish commitment and service to Yah and his people have demonstrated to me the most perfect example of fealty and dedication I have ever witnessed. I have benefited enormously from him being my leader, teacher, brother and personal friend, so much so, that words are inadequate to express my profound gratitude and appreciation.

This book is also dedicated to the eternal memory of my spiritual father, His Excellency Prince Shaleahk Ben Yehuda, Prince Chancellor and Dean of The School of The Prophets at Jerusalem. He has consistently represented the righteous spirit of Divine intellect in the midst of the people. He caused

14

me to realize the importance of injecting the wisdom of Yah into the hearts and minds of the people through literary works. This was a prime motivating factor in bringing this book into existence. To him I shall always be eternally grateful.

I further dedicate these writings to the living memory of "The Elder Priest," Prince Eleaser. As a founding father of the Divine Prophetic Priesthood at Jerusalem, he contributed invaluably to this work by helping to create and perpetuate Divine Marriage as a viable institution within this dispensation of time. His great works as well as the ongoing work of the Prophetic Priesthood in this arena have provided the perfect model as a foundation for this book.

Lastly, I want to dedicate this book to The Honorable Ben Ammi, Anointed Spiritual Leader of the Hebrew Israelites of Jerusalem. His unwavering stand for Yah and the law have catapulted the world into the Messianic Kingdom Age. I have been blessed to be a part of the Kingdom which he has fathered. This is the foundation on which I stand, without which these writings could not have come forth. My prayer is that this work will be of assistance to him in his great work of bringing about the rebirth of the righteous for the Kingdom of Yah.

"(Yeshua) answered, and said unto him, verily, verily I say unto thee, Except a man be born again, he cannot see the kingdom of (Yah)." "For the kingdom of (Yah) is not food and drink, but righteousness, and peace, and joy in the Holy Spirit."

John 3:3 / Romans 14:17

About The Author

Dr. Haraymiel Ben Shaleahk[1] was born on August 22, 1947 to Gilbert and Lydia in Chicago, Illinois, and was the fifth of eight children. Haraymiel and I met in 1959 when my high school friendship with one of his sisters provided me an opportunity to spend a lot of time at their home. In a short period of time, I was considered a part of the family.

Haraymiel began high school on Chicago's west side later transferring to another school on the south side. He left high school after two years and joined the U.S. Army, Paratrooper Corps, serving in both Germany and Vietnam. During his time in the military we were married, beginning 39 years of joy and high adventure. In 1970, he received an honorable discharge and once again became a civilian. Although, both tours were very demanding, especially Vietnam, he easily readjusted to civilian life, unlike so many veterans of that conflict.

Though the effects of his military experience never really left his awareness, he transformed the experience into a positive motivation for change, redirecting his energies to becoming a good husband, father and community activist. This was not the first demonstration of his individual strength of character. Haraymiel, was extraordinary from his youth. His intelligence allowed him to master whatever he decided he wanted to do and he has always been exceptionally articulate. In addition, Haraymiel is a kind, considerate and sensitive person, always seeking ways to help others. I always knew he was destined for great things.

Having attained relative stability in his work, family and social interaction, he was still unsatisfied and continued searching for something more in life. When he joined the Black Christian Nationalists, the movement reflected some of his consciousness, but not enough. During his season of searching, our family experienced something new everyday. While attending Malcolm X College under the GI bill, he met a brother[2] named Voo-el. It was Voo-el who introduced him to the Hebrew Israelite philosophy and taught Haraymiel that the Bible was a history book and that African Americans are among the descendants of the people of the Bible.

Before meeting Voo-el, Haraymiel was a certified agnostic. So, naturally the curiosity of our family and friends was aroused when he came home and told us about his biblical discovery. Haraymiel arranged a meeting with Voo-el and the family. From that meeting, our lives began to change. We became vegetarians, our dress became more modest and African, and Haraymiel began studying the Bible.

Soon thereafter, Haraymiel announced that as free African people we should be returning to Mother Africa and to prepare to move to Liberia. I said to myself, "This is just another one of his phases". I really did not think it was actually going to happen until he began to sell the furniture. We moved into a smaller place (his brother's attic) so that all of our funds could be channeled into moving to Liberia, West Africa. My love and faith in him increased phenomenally, for as the process unfolded, he became more confident and self-assured in his commitment. In December of 1975, we left America with our two daughters, Ahaviah and Neiyah.

The entire family, except Haraymiel, went through a period of adjustment. But he displayed so much faith and confidence that it soon made all of us comfortable with his decision. Within weeks, he was gainfully employed in Liberia. During our first two years, Haraymiel worked as a site manager for two major construction companies and a supervisor with Liberia's National Housing Authority.

In 1977, Prince Asiel, the International Ambassador of the Hebrew Israelites of Jerusalem, came to Liberia. Having been told that some African Americans were living there, he saught us out. When Haraymiel met Prince Asiel, he was extremely impressed and was the first of our group to gravitate to the great truth represented by the Prince and his community in Israel. Subsequently, in the tradition of his pioneering spirit, Haraymiel quickly became an intricate part of the development of the Liberian extension of the Hebrew Israelite Community.

Later, Haraymiel established his own construction company, which not only employed the Hebrew brothers but the indigenous people as well. The company was not only noted for constructing large infrastructural projects such as roads and bridges but also private houses and schools at affordable prices. This gave the company the reputation of being "builders with a heart." In addition to managing the construction company, Haraymiel lectured on various topics including history, biblical studies, male/female relations, child rearing, health and nutrition.

After twelve years on the Liberian frontier, Haraymiel was reassigned to the United States, where he worked in Chicago, Washington, D.C. and New Orleans. Once again, he showed his versatility by earning his doctorate degree at night while overseeing the Hebrew Israelite Defense Fund by day.

The Legal Defense Fund was formed in response to a legal campaign mounted against the community and its leadership, in an effort to discredit and destroy the emerging Hebrew Israelite movement worldwide, including its settlement in Israel, Northeast Africa. Haraymiel was responsible for organizing many of the sit-ins, all-night vigils, protest marches and telethons that assisted in ultimately winning greater recognition of the community's plight in Israel.

Since returning home to the Holy Land, he has exemplified the same tenacity, creativity and fortitude that is reflected in his life-long achievements in helping to build the community of the Hebrew Israelites of Jerusalem. Most notably, he has turned his attention to Divine Agriculture and the institution of Divine Marriage, both fundamental building blocks of this visionary New World Family, being fashioned by these brave pioneers.

As a result of Haraymiel applying the Old Testament teachings concerning the expanded family, we married my sister-wife, Gheliyah, opening a new realm of spirituality and love in our family. Since then we have married my newest sister-wife, Yahlee. Currently, Haraymiel is the CEO of his own production and management company and is studying to become a natural doctor. He also serves as Marketing Manager for the organic farm project of the Hebrew Community and offers marriage counseling services via his internet website.

Reviewing the background of the author will help the reader to understand why this book will stand out as one of the essential tools for reconfiguring the social, cultural and spiritual mindset of all people to the mandate of Yah. The concepts presented here by Dr. Shaleahk will help to effectively move us into the twenty-first century.

Without Pretense is a wake-up call for a shift of perception, from the old to the new paradigm of the Yah centered family order and lifestyle. Dr. Shaleahk's experience and insight will be treasured for years to come.

Nasiyah Eshet Dr. Haraymiel Ben Shaleahk

[1]Among the Hebrew Israelites, all names have a specific meaning relating to attributes of Yah. Receiving a name, therefore, is a privilege and a sign of confirmatiom within the community. The name Haraymiel means, "The elevated of Yah" in the Hebrew language, Ben means "son" and Shaleahk is the name of his spiritual father. [2]The term "Brother" is used in the colloquial sense of "soul brother".

Foreword

... And, when the handsome prince married the beautiful princess, they lived happily ever after. Love, peace, happiness and eternal marital bliss; is it all a fairy tale, or does it only happen in the movies?

Unlike the dramas of Snow White and Cinderella, life in today's world often renders unfavorable scenarios. In this high-tech, hyper-space age where drugs, crime and immorality run rampant; rather than search the kingdom for the fair maiden whose foot fit the golden slipper, the corrupt, "modern day" prince would more likely opt to pawn the lovely shoe for a "bag of crack."

So, after nine years of a former marriage, an acrimonious divorce and five years of being "the other woman" in one bad relationship after another, I, like millions of other women in America's monogamous society, drew the harsh conclusion that when it came to relationships and marriage, it all boiled down to two basic questions: *"What's love got to do with it?"* and *"What have you done for me lately?"*

Looking at today's rising divorce rate and increasing number of single parent homes, we can clearly see that divorce rather than marriage has become the way of life and that no one really expects love or relationships to last forever.

> Increasingly over the last quarter-century, as women expand their careers, marriage rates have fallen and divorce rates have increased. In the United States, the statistics per 1,000 couples surveyed reveals, the marriage rate has gone from 10.5 to 9.8 and the divorce rate from 3.7 to

4.7, reflecting a 10% marriage decrease and a 25% divorce increase. Figures worldwide per 1,000 couples surveyed indicate a 35% marriage decline and an astounding 78% divorce increase.

National Center For Policy Analysis

The truth of these realities is so grim and devastating that we must search within ourselves and ask: "Is this what (Yah) wants for us?" How do we end this vicious cycle? Can a more promising and positive foundation be instituted for our children? Will our prayers for family unity, happiness and security be answered in our lifetime? Is there hope for establishing and maintaining better relationships and family dynamics? At last, answers to these pertinent questions and the solutions to problems that have sorely abridged the quality of our lives can be found within the pages of **Without Pretense**.

Who are our women, sisters, daughters, grand daughters, nieces and cousins going to marry? With the bureau of vital statistics reporting far more female births than males worldwide, and so many men, particularly in the African American community, in jail, on drugs, dying at an early age or homosexual, how is it numerically possible for every woman to have a husband? From where do the eligible grooms come?

Many women have attempted to satisfy their need for companionship by focusing on their careers, turning to the church, to lesbianism or having affairs with married men. Are these options in accordance with (Yah's) Divine Will and purpose for the "rib" he took from man? **Absolutely not!** Halleluyah, Dr. Shaleahk has courageously come forth to resolve the multiple-wife controversy once and for all, proving unquestionably that, *more than one wife is the marital system ordained and sanctioned by (Yah)!*

The world needs to take a serious look at the marital systems it has instituted, to assess the unhappiness and trauma it has caused in the lives of its inhabitants. It is obvious that both the monogamous and polygenous systems, as we know them today, are not working.

Without Pretense graphically illustrates how the lack of discernment is the principal cause of most of today's problems, especially regarding marriage. For without (Yah), any government or society and its accompanying social and marital systems are destined to fail. Because changes are so desperately needed, Dr. Shaleahk presents the proven precepts of Divine Marriage as the only wholesome and viable alternative for ensuring the perpetuation and well being of our posterity.

Without Pretense provides clear and practical applications for establishing and maintaining the most vital components required for life, love and happiness in the relationships of men and women. After ten years of marriage to Dr. Shaleahk, my sister-wife Nasiyah, (who've been married 39 years) and my newest sister-wife, Yahlee, of two years, I can unequivocally testify that love, peace, happiness and eternal marital bliss are attainable realities for those who earnestly apply the principles discussed in **Without Pretense.**

Work is required, but joyous results are guaranteed for those who are diligently seeking to achieve, improve and maintain Divine and Holy Relationships. To live and enjoy the vast benefits of Divine Marriage, as thoroughly explained in this fascinating book, is truly a blessing. Actually experiencing two or more women harmoniously sharing the same house, and openly loving and being loved by the same man is achievable. Witnessing a man who sensitively attends to the needs of his wives and family and consciously strives to abide by the laws of (Yah), is indeed marvelous work to behold.

More wonderful than a fairy tale and grander than a big screen movie; **Without Pretense** emphatically demonstrates that there is nothing more fulfilling than "everyone getting what they need in a relationship …**Divinely."**

Gheliyah Eshet Dr. Haraymiel Ben Shaleahk

Preface

Male/female relations are a major concern of every society in the world today. Divorces and separations are a normal part of every day life and have become the rule as opposed to the exception. Many people, both young and old, are completely lost when it comes to understanding how to develop and maintain a fulfilling marital relationship and often end up merely acting out the part. Most do not know what to look for in a mate, and among those who think they do or are not willing to admit that they don't, often find themselves unable to find a suitable prospect.

Therefore, fewer and fewer people are getting married. More and more are electing instead, to simply live together, so they can exit easily when the inevitable breakup occurs. Those possessing any kind of wealth and who still believe in getting married, are more likely than not to obtain some kind of pre-nuptial agreement before taking the vows. Despite their desires and positive attitude, they too don't really expect the marriage to last. An entire generation has grown into adulthood without experiencing the strength, security and love that comes with being part of a stable family and the results are horrendous.

> Of the 10,000,000 households surveyed in 1997 5,000,000 households consisted of unmarried couples of opposite sexes.

Nat'l. Bureau of Vital Statistics, 1997

The zest and vitality which emanate from a secure and loving relationship, have gone from the lives of many, only to be replaced by temporary lust and uncommitted copulation. How do we restore this essential element of life? Is there any hope or are we to forever be faced with this seemingly unstoppable downward spiral, as the deepening crisis continues? It is time to stop the pretense. For the answers to these and many other plaguing relationship related questions, we must turn back to Yah, the source of all blessings. Having been blessed to receive a portion of these blessings from my teachers, research and experiences, I am compelled by Yah's spirit, to share them with you.

It is therefore, with the utmost humility that I undertake this writing. First, I recognize the magnitude and importance of such a treatise. Secondly, I am more than aware of the need for a clear and concise discourse on this subject. Finally, I understand, full well, the impact this will have in the lives of those who use this guide. I will be stating in unequivocal terms, the absolute truth concerning the issues being discussed because I realize that only truth can deliver us from the morass of lies and deceit in which this world has placed the family of man.

"Neither do men light a candle, and put it under a bushel, but on a candlestick; and it giveth light unto all that are in the house. Let your light so shine before men, that they may see your good works, and glorify your Father, who is in heaven."

Matthew 5:15-16

Much of the information and analysis of which this book is comprised, has been culled and developed during more than thirty years of observation, discussions and counseling sessions with various Saints (individual community members), Princes (Holy Governing Council Members), Ministers (chief community administrators), the Priesthood (principle spiritual counselors and teachers of the law) and, especially, the teachings of Ben Ammi (The Anointed Spiritual Leader).

As a result of this effort and the personal experience gained by applying and or painfully, not applying these principles in my own life and marriage, I can now share these truths with you. I ask, as you read this book, that you open your mind, humble your spirit and prepare yourself to receive these keys. They will unlock the doors to a better understanding, which will enable you to enter into a Divine Relationship; a relationship that will be both fulfilling and everlasting.

Within these pages we will address in a clear and understandable manner, the male/female relationship questions most needing to be answered. And, if we only succeed in raising other questions that stimulate broader dialogue and thus, pre-empt or resolve relationship conflicts and their resulting trauma, then we say, "All praises to Yah," our objective has been achieved.

These writings are based on the marital system of the Kingdom of Yah and to a large degree, will be readily useable by it's citizens. However, the truths and laws of Yah are universal and govern the lives of everyone. I am therefore confident, that all those truly seeking legitimate, honest and workable marital relationships that flourish "Without Pretense" and are willing to humble themselves to the will of Yah, will find the keys they need within these pages.

We shall explore how to begin a relationship that will remain a source of joy for the participants as well as how to repair one that is floundering in the sea of despair. Utilizing the Holy marital model provided by the Hebrew Community, we will chart the road map, which anyone can follow to a joyously Divine Marriage. I pray this book proves to be a blessing to you and your loved ones.

The Holy Art Of Divine Marriage

Art is at the root of many aspects of man and his endeavors to express himself. There are the fine arts, represented by those skilled in the production of beautiful sculptures, paintings, jewelry, etc. We then have the performing arts, represented by great singers, dancers, musicians, actors, etc. There are also branches of higher learning or educational disciplines such as liberal arts and the humanities, and there are of course, many other art forms to which men apply their time, energies and resources.

However, regardless of the particular form, central themes do exist which act as common denominators to make art, Art. These include creativity, skill, a system of rules or methods of performing particular actions relative to the desired result and lastly, knowledge and it's proper application. Others likewise exist and are relevant to a greater or lesser degree depending on the particular art form. The Holy Art of which we speak, Divine Marriage, requires all of the aforementioned denominators plus some additional ones. Principal among them are:

1. **Faith in Yah** (the knowledge that Yah is just and His word infallible.)
2. **Lawful spirit** (a love for the instructions of Yah and a commitment to live by them.)
3. **Respect Yah's preferred order** (Yah, man, woman, children.)
4. **Submitting to Yah** (being fashioned and guided by His order.)
5. **Divine love and patience**
6. **Honesty and sensitivity**
7. **Willingness to work at making it right**

As we know, artists dedicate their entire lives to creating and perfecting mere inanimate art pieces. These are sometimes sold for great sums and are often considered valued treasures. How much more would we give for a Holy, Yah inspired living art treasure? What is the value of a Holy Institution that would provide for the continuity of life and the foundation for all our happiness? How much harder would we work to obtain it? How much more value would we place on such a work of art?

By referring to Divine Marriage as a Holy Art, it is my prayer that the reader will recognize from the outset, that a "Divine Marriage" is something of tremendous value. Something which requires serious personal involvement to establish and even greater dedication and commitment to maintain. Additionally, this institution is, whether you are aware of it or not, governed by Yah's immutable laws which cannot be violated.

Such an art cannot be mastered unless you are prepared to face the truth and stop living your life as though lies, deceit and pretense can bring about the blessings you seek. With this understanding, one is prepared to go forth to build a Divine Relationship.

Chapter 1:
Is It Real Or Is It Memorex?

A Question Of Discernment

It is sometimes difficult for those, who exist within the matrix of so called "modern society" to understand the principles regarding Divine Marriage. This is because they have been the victims of satan's disinformation campaign against Yah and don't possess the gift of discernment. Discernment is a special gift from Yah, that is only given to those who humbly submit and seek to do His will.

It does not matter into what area of life we look, if you are not seeking to please Yah, you will not be able to properly discern the dynamics involved. You will see but not see, hear but not hear, know but not know. The lack of discernment, is the single most serious obstruction, hampering the proper development of Divine Relationships.

"But the natural man receiveth not the things of the Spirit of (Yah); for they are foolishness unto him, neither can he know them, because they are spiritually discerned."

I Corinthians 2:14

When we, either as a people or as individuals, humbly submit to the will of Yah and seek to be pleasing unto Him, Yah rewards us with the ability to discern. It is only with discernment capabilities that we are able to properly digest and evaluate the things we perceive with our senses or more especially through the spirit. Possessing the gift of discernment is very important in all areas of life, but it is crucial to Divine Relationships. Here are some common examples of possessing or not possessing this precious gift.

When a woman has a baby and her breasts become heavy with milk, it does not take a rocket scientist to understand the proper relationship between the baby and those breasts. Yet, without the gift of discernment, even the rocket scientist, despite his intellect, will go to the supermarket to buy cow's milk or Similac for his baby. The fact that cow's milk was designed for the particular developmental needs of a baby cow and that human milk was designed for human babies shouldn't be too difficult to understand. However, without discernment, this is extremely difficult to understand, for some, even impossible.

A calf has to be capable of walking moments after birth and requires extra-strong bones to do so. This could account for why Yah put so much calcium (a bone building element) in the cow's milk the calf was to drink. A human baby on the other hand, spends the first year of its life basically lying down, watching and learning a host of crucial things. This makes intellectual perception a critical component to his early development.

\ Could this need for superior intellect be the reason Yah put so much vitamin B-12, zinc and iron (brain developing elements) in the mother's milk that her baby was to drink?

We can reasonably attribute many of the behavioral, health and learning problems children suffer to the consumption of cow's milk instead of their mother's milk. A mother possessing the gift of discernment will automatically breast feed her child. Even if she doesn't know why her milk is better for her baby, she will discern that it is.

I'm going into more detail concerning cow's milk because it is so destructive, so unecessary and yet so widely used through out the world. Please indulge me in this as a more perfect example of lack of discernment would be difficult to find. In their book "Fit For Life II" Doctors Harvey and Marilyn Diamond expound as follows:

> ### THE CASE AGAINST DAIRY PRODUCTS
> It is outright misrepresentation and commercialism to perpetuate the ridiculous belief that we can't meet our protein needs without eating animal products.
>
> I'd sure love to watch those of you who disagree chase down a rabbit, tear it apart with your teeth and hands (if you could catch it), and devour it raw: blood, guts, bones, skin, flesh, and all just as any genuine, self-respecting flesh eater would. And after finishing off the rabbit, I'd like to watch you go out into a pasture, get down on all fours, and suck the milk out of a cow's udder to wash the dead rabbit down.

That's a little repulsive, too, isn't it? Why? Because it is not our natural inclination. If you didn't get the milk from your own mother's breast, it's too late! The fact is that the majority of people on earth react to cow's milk by getting sick. It's an insult to nature's grand scheme to go to another species for milk.

There is a reason why all mammals have milk available at the birth of their young. It is because each species' milk is uniquely beneficial for that species. That's nature! That is why two things are true for every mammal on earth except us:

1. They do not consume the milk of another species. That would mean crossing over their biological adaptation, and they don't do that. (Remember, we're not talking about pets or animals in zoos, whom we have managed to pervert as much as ourselves.)

2. Once weaned, no animal ever again consumes milk. Milk is the food designed by nature to feed the young of the species. It is specifically designed for the rapid growth of an infant. That is what it is for! It is idiocy to insist we continue drinking it after infancy, to drink it into our eighties, if we can get that far. The ridiculousness of it is lamentable. Do we actually believe that as our mothers finish cows should begin?

How is it that the species with the most sophisticated brain, the greatest intelligence and the unique ability to reason is too dense to see this simple truth? And then there's the ironic fact that Dairy Products Are Disease-Producing. They're harmful. They cause suffering. They're the perfect thing to eat if you want to be sick and have a diseased body.

Cow's milk is designed to quickly create a huge, big-boned animal with four stomachs, and there's no way humans meet those criteria (although, unfortunately, I have seen some people who are starting to look dangerously close).

Consider this: Cow's milk is designed to take an infant calf, weighing 90 pounds at birth, to a weight of 2000 pounds in only two years. Human infants weigh 6 to 8 pounds at birth and will attain a weight of only 100 to 200 pounds in eighteen years! Eating dairy products is eating food designed by nature to make you very big, like a cow, very fast.

If you're presently eating dairy products, I hope you're not trying to lose weight. You'd have a better chance of putting out a fire by throwing kerosene on it. But there is so much more that is harmful about dairy products that I hardly know where to start.

Cow's milk causes more mucus than any food you can eat- thick, dense mucus that clogs and irritates the body and prevents the fluid operation of the system; dense, gluey mucus that places a tremendous burden on the eliminative faculties of the body, clogs the delicate mucous membranes and invites disease.

Hay fever, asthma, bronchitis, sinusitis, colds, runny noses, and ear infections are all primarily caused by dairy products. Dairy products are the leading cause of allergies. Practically every book, every paper, every study that discusses allergies implicates dairy products.

There simply is no question of its role in this area. Despite overwhelming scientific fact, basic common sense, and clear logic, successful advertising by the dairy industry and the promptings of dietitians and nutritionists hired by them have somehow convinced us that calves' food is essential for human survival.

There are two elements in dairy products that have to be broken down by enzymes in the body: lactose and casein. Lactose is broken down by the enzyme lactase, and casein is broken down by the enzyme rennin. By age three or four rennin is nonexistent in the human digestive tract and, in all but a small number of people, so is lactase.

The term lactose intolerance is thrown around as if it were some rare occurrence that manifests only on occasion. In fact, over 98 percent of the population is lactose intolerant, for they have no lactase.

Casein is the protein component in milk. It is a very thick, coarse substance and used to make one of the strongest wood glues known. Glue sandwich, anyone? There is 300 percent more casein in cow's milk than in human milk. The by-products of the bacterial decomposition of casein end up in thick, ropelike mucus that sticks to mucous membranes and clogs our bodies. The human body plainly has no digestive mechanisms to break it down.

Sudden infant death syndrome (SIDS) is a particularly heart-breaking tragedy. A small, innocent newborn baby goo-gooing and gaa-gaaing one moment is dead the next. While SIDS can't be blamed on any one cause, dairy products are unquestionably partially to blame. I realize that bit of information will not make mothers very happy, especially those who have unfortunately lost their child to SIDS, but the evidence is there and it must be looked at.

Were it not for modern technology, all mammals would simply feed their young, and, once weaned, all would then go on to exist on the foods they are biologically adapted to.

In the wild, milk drinking is not an issue; it is only an issue for that one mammal too "smart" to trust nature's plan.

Fit For Life II
by Harvey and Marilyn Diamond, M.D.

Cancer Earned Is Cancer Gained

It is more than obvious, when we examine the facts surrounding milk that a serious lack of discernment exist. Another clear example of the need for discernment and the lack thereof, is illustrated by cigarette smokers. It's common knowledge that smoking cigarettes causes cancer and kills people. It kills, not in a quick merciful manner (if any murder can be considered merciful) but slowly and agonizingly with great pain and the constant erosion of the quality of life.

Despite this devastation, not only do people smoke, but they also give cigarettes to the people they love. Even doctors, who treat cancer patients and see first hand, the misery suffered by smokers and their families, continue to smoke.

People endure all kinds of hardships, just for a smoke. For instance, in America during the dead of winter, people who work in "smoke free" buildings, where smoking is not permitted, stand outside in freezing rain and snow just to smoke. They know they're slowly destroying themselves, but being totally void of discernment, they say "you've got to die from something" and therefore smoke anyway. And if this isn't bad enough, they pay their hard earned money for the privilege. Discernment would cause them to see all this folly and abandon smoking.

> Let us draw from an example of a victim who has lung cancer caused by cigarette smoking. How did he arrive at such a horrendous end? First of all, he had to work to earn money to purchase his cigarettes because they are not given away.

Secondly, he had to walk or drive to a location which sells the little packs. Thirdly, he had to open his pack, remove the object, place it in his mouth, take out his little fire stick and light his cigarette. He then puffed, inhaled and exhaled smoke. He had to go through this process not just one day, one month or even one year; he performed this ritual with intense regularity for long periods of time.

Moreover, and most ironic, is the fact that the conclusion of this process was known by the victim at the onset. What does this individual merit from God for his supreme effort to destroy his temple? How easy it would have been to just not smoke and thereby be healthy! In truth, the victim has earned the right to his lung cancer after such a tremendous effort.

God the Black Man and Truth
by Ben Ammi, Communicators Press

The many situations surrounding cigarette smoking are, for the most part, so ludicrous that if it weren't so terribly tragic, it would be down right hilarious. Think for a moment, governments and "health oriented institutions" like the prestigious American Medical Association, which have at their disposal some of the most brilliant minds of our time, have thus far been unable to find a cure for lung cancer.

They've spent billions of dollars and years of research, not to mention millions of lives, pursuing this cause to no avail. Because they have no discernment, they can't figure out that the only cure is to outlaw cigarettes and air pollution and this cure is absolutely free.

According to a 1977 American Cancer Society report: 57,535 female deaths were caused by lung cancer. The society also reports: an alarming 91,825 male deaths were caused by lung cancer in one year.

American Cancer Society

Meanwhile, the offending society attempts to bury or conceal its guilt. Let us consider how the cigarette manufacturers attempt to conceal their criminal offense by offering you its great all around "life insurance policy." "Complete coverage" they call it. You are so beguiled and blinded by these "benefits" that you cannot see the true criminal or his victims.

The multi-national R. J. Reynolds cigarette manufacturers (whose assets were the objective of a $25 billion corporate take-over recently) also provide life insurance policies. To be sure, the company also contributes large sums to cancer research – as if they
did not know that cigarettes are inextricably linked to cancer and are destroying your health (life)!

Reynolds and other cigarette manufacturers brazenly write this on their (your) package, gambling that in spite of the warnings, their policies, contributions and seductions (advertisements) will keep you blinded to the fact that they are criminals and you are their victims. So, they go on providing compensation for what they are causing, certain you are going to need it ; powerlessly caught up as you are in the unrighteous cycles of death.

God the Black Man and Truth
by Ben Ammi, Communicators Press

How can advertisement companies continue to promote smoking as some kind of panacea to be sought after and then as a reward, make such suggestions as; "You've come a long
way baby" or "Come to Marlboro Country?" How can governments that purport to represent the people, continue to allow the production and sale of such highly lethal products to the public? Why is there no significant outcry from the people? The answer is simple, the lack of discernment. To further ensure the reader's grasp of the need for and benefit of discernment, I offer the following illustrations.

The Alleged War On Drugs

There is an alleged international multi-government war on drugs. We are told that everything possible is being done to stop the flow of drugs. It is a well established fact that the drugs being used in cities the world over are not being grown in those cities, but are brought in from specific places which are known. Occasionally, someone will slip up and mistakenly cause exposure of governmental involvement in the international drug trade, such as the Oliver North Case.

You might remember the American military plane, loaded with drugs and guns that was shot down over Nicaragua by a Sandinista soldier. A baggage handler named Eugene Hasenfuse was the only survivor. This incident led to the exposure of the White House's involvment in importing drugs for sale to help fund the Contra war in Nicaragua.

Some of the natural questions that were never raised were: What real efforts would drug dealers put forth to stop drug traffic? How could Oliver North, who, ran this drug-Contra operation as a "National Security Advisor," go on to become a national hero with all its accompanying accolades and benefits? And, how did everyone forget that the drugs he sold killed people? Simply, a failure to discern.

The next natural question would be; looking at the life of a drug addict, who would want to aspire to become one? Perhaps children who don't know better. But what about the rich and well educated, famous athletes and entertainers, the corporate, political and social leaders who let drugs ruin their lives? Surely, they know better. It all goes back to not possessing the gift of discernment. They are unable to assess things in a manner that would cause them to respond differently.

According to the Substance Abuse and Mental Health Services Administration's 1997 national survey, of an estimated 77 million Americans 12 years of age and older, 36% had used an illicit drug at least once during their lifetimes. Among those 25 years of age and under, an estimated 1.6 million used cocaine (including crack) and 9.7 million used marijuana at least once within the previous year.

Among those 26 years and over, 2.6 million used cocaine (including crack) and 9.7 million used marijuana at least once within the previous year.

**Substance Abuse and Mental
Health Administration**

When Does Life Begin?

Another glaring example of no discernment is noted when we examine the issue of abortion. A heated debate has been raging for many years concerning this subject. What lies at the center of the abortion issue is the simple question of, when does life begin? Anti-abortion factions contend that it ranges from the time of conception to two or three months into the gestation period, depending on to whom you're listening. The pro-abortion factions place the beginning of life anywhere from the fourth month until the actual birth, again depending on who's talking.

Both factions seem to miss the fact that when a man and a woman come together, the sperm cell he deposits is already alive and the egg cell from the woman, with which it unites is likewise already alive. This being the case, how can there be an argument about when life begins? It should be obvious that life began long before the man and woman came together.

Due to the fact that the societies which are arguing the issue are not seeking to please Yah, they are not blessed with the ability to discern even the obvious. They are seeking instead, to circumvent Yah and murder the unborn while pretending to do right. Just as in the search for the cancer cure, they want to continue to smoke and circumvent the laws of Yah and not suffer the consequences of their violations. Truly there is no discernment or humility in them.

"Humble yourselves in the sight of the Lord, and He shall lift you up."

James 4:10

Because this world is literally crammed with similar examples, we could dedicate several volumes to this subject alone and still only scratch the surface. Since that is not the purpose of this writing, I won't dwell on this issue. The point I want to make however, is that this same lack of discernment is prevalent in most people's perceptions concerning marital relations.

We must return to the original position of man, which is to seek through our humble submission to be pleasing to Yah and thereby receive the blessed gift of discernment. This will enable us to correctly perceive and discern all things including the proper marital system, the one Yah designed for us, in order to fulfill His Divine Will. It is through humble eyes that we are to observe the creation and learn the ways of Yah. Yah teaches us in many ways. He gives us numerous examples to emulate so that His path will be easy to find and follow.

A Yah-less World Gone Wrong

This world, through its arrogance and "Yah-less" agenda has lost its way and is heading down all the wrong paths. It promotes the eating of the wrong foods, so the hospitals and grave yards are full of those who have suffered the consequences. It promotes the wearing of the wrong clothes, so women parade around half nude and become rape victims. It promotes the wrong moral and social values, so drugs proliforate, crime escalates and promiscuity abounds.

> Of the estimated 265,284,000 population reported by the Bureau of Census, there were 95,770 reported cases of forcible rape and 1,682,280 cases of violent crime reported in the U.S. in one year.
>
> **FBI, Uniform Crime Report**

How can we believe that a world that has gone so wrong, in every possible way, would be right in its institutional design for male/female relationships and marriage?

Especially, when we observe the overwhelming number of marriages that either end in divorce, spousal murder or simple separation. While many of those that remain in existence, do so for the wrong reasons, i.e., children, economics, convenience or fear of being alone. The ability to discern tells us that this is due to the incorrectness of the system and the values it represents.

When we are instructed by Yah through our humble observation of His creation, we learn valuable lessons which can help us understand His plans for us. How do we know when Yah wants us to go to sleep? He will turn out His light (the sun) and our bodies will get tired. How do we know when Yah wants us to eat? He will cause our stomachs to rumble and feel empty. How does a new mother know what Yah wants her to feed her baby? He will fill her breast with milk and the baby will go for it.

All these things occur naturally and our humility and discernment cause us to acknowledge them and submit to them. It should be noted, that not only does Yah instruct us in what we should do but at the same time He provides the means by which we can do it. In many instances, the fact that something exists as a means, will be the indicator of its usage.

As in the example of the manifestation of the mother's milk after the birth of a baby: its presence not only tells us what the baby should be fed but it is also the actual food Yah is providing us to give to the baby. Understanding this principle provides a vital key in helping you make the correct choices between, what Yah would have you do and what the anti-Yah forces would have you think that Yah wants you to do.

51

Utilizing the same example of the mother's milk; we find that Yah intended one thing and provided the means; but we are taught instead, that cow's milk should be our children's food. Without discernment and understanding, the whole world is drinking cow's milk. Not only do the children suffer but so do the mothers. Much of the breast cancer in women can be attributed to their not using the breast for its intended purpose.

> According to the 1977 American Cancer Society's report: 43,644 women died of breast cancer; 4,602 women died of cervical cancer; 13,500 women died of ovarian cancer; 28,936 women died of colon cancer and 57,535 female deaths were caused by lung cancer. Numerous drugs that may prevent breast cancer or improve its treatment are being studied.

> One is tamoxifen, a synthetic hormone that blocks the action of estrogen in the breast. Already used for treating breast cancer, it has been shown to reduce the likelihood of developing the disease in women who are considered high risk. Unfortunately, tamoxifen also has dangerous side effects, such as increased risk of uterine cancer and blood clots in the lungs.

American Cancer Society, 1999

"DISCERNMENT PRECEDES LIFE, BLINDNESS IS DEATH ITSELF"

The masses of the people have been blinded to the truth and are victims of a world rotating on the axis of a lie. To attain sustained happiness, on any level, particularly in a marital relationship, **YOU MUST COME TO GRIPS WITH THE FOLLOWING FACTS:**

1. There is a need for sight, because you have been blinded.

2. Your blindness is not coincidental, but contrived, so you will be unable to see the evil traps that have been set for you.

3. Anti-Yah forces have constructed these traps, from the lies which govern your perspective on everything and therefore, your very life.

4. Fully accept the fact that **SIGHT IS, "THE ABILITY TO DISCERN"** and can **ONLY** be obtained by humbly submitting to the will of Yah.

5. The same force that deceives you about, food, cigarettes, abortions, cow's milk, drugs(both legal and illegal) etc. also deceives you concerning proper marital relationships.

6. You must call into question all you have been taught about life and living and most especially about love and marriage.

7. It doesn't matter how long you've believed a thing or how often you've done it, if it's based on a lie you must gain enough discernment to see it and enough strength to change it.

53

"And the great dragon was cast out, that old serpent, called the Devil and Satan, who deceiveth the whole world; he was cast out into the earth, and his angels were cast out with him."

Revelation 12:9

Chapter 2
Which System Of Marriage
Monogamy, Polygyny Or Divine?

A Comparative Analysis

Should a woman be permitted to marry into a family where a wife or wives already exist? Should a man be permitted to marry more than one woman? Is having more than one wife correct or incorrect? Is it just or unjust, sanctioned or abhorrent to Yah? What is "Divine Marriage?" **THESE ARE THE QUESTIONS OF THE DAY, WHICH MUST BE ANSWERED** and answered both truthfully and sincerely.

This subject is being covered at this early stage, because the contextual nature of much of our later discussions will be more easily understood with this foundation already established.

Not only is it necessary to know and understand what Divine Marriage is, but equally important, in view of all the misconceptions, we must know what Divine Marriage is not.

First and foremost, it should be understood that "Divine Marriage" is one thing and "polygyny" is quite another. Though both have some similar components, it is the differences rather than the similarities that more than anything else, describe and determine the character of each marital system. These distinctions are the points to be focused on when one is attempting to understand them. We can easily discern these character distinctions by examining the definitions of each system.

"Polygyny," (not to be confused with polygamy) is a marital system wherein a man can take more than one wife and a woman can marry a man that is already married, but can only have one husband; as opposed to "Monogamy" which only permits one spouse, be it the husband or the wife. Though most polygynous societies are African or eastern and the monogamous societies are primarily western, neither is necessarily Yah centered. Even though eastern societies do lean more toward Yah consciousness with polygynous marital systems than western societies do with monogamy, the fact remains, that many of the permissible practices of each are distinctly anti-Yah.

In a Divine Marriage like a polygynous one, a man can have more than one wife, as ordained by Yah. Divine Marriage however, unlike both monogamy and polygyny, is based entirely on fulfilling the plan and adhering to the will of Yah. For instance, one of the fundamental mandates Yah gave man was to "be fruitful and multiply and replenish the earth." For man, this was not merely a command to physically procreate but was also a spiritual mandate to reproduce righteousness and the intellect of Yah in all things, throughout the creation.

"And (Yah) blessed them, and said unto them, Be fruitful, and multiply, and fill the earth, and subdue it; and have dominion over the fish of the sea, and the fowl of the air, and over every living thing that moveth upon the earth."

Genesis 1:28

To effectively carry out this directive, man needs help and help in abundance. The perfection of Yah is such, that He wouldn't give you a charge and then deny you the means by which to accomplish it. Thus, He created woman as a helpmate fit for man and He did so abundantly. This allows man to multiply his seed and the righteousness of Yah, in order to replenish the earth.

In addition to needing help to fulfill the mandate of Yah, man also needs the desire to be pleasing to Yah in all things. Complying with the instructions "to be fruitful and multiply," is but one area of man's life in which he must strive to be pleasing to Yah. His intense desire to comply, will cause him to diligently search for correctness, and through these efforts, Yah will bless him with the gift of discernment. This discernment will help him to know what is intended by Yah relative to the questions regarding relationships and marriage.

The mandate from Yah "to be fruitful and multiply" was given to man but not to man alone. It was also given to all other living things in the creation. Additionally, a particular means was also given to each through which it could comply, according to the parameters of its particular mandate. Every living thing in the creation humbly submits to fulfilling its mandate except man. As a result, there is a level of confusion, suffering and pain in man's life, that is not experienced by any other creature in the universe.

This particular mandate relates directly to the institution of marriage and can help provide an understanding of what it is meant to do in the creation. When we are clear on what role Yah planned marriage to play, we are then able to discern what provisions He made for the manifestation of that plan.

Multiple Wives: The Issue In Perspective

At this point we can use our discernment to observe the creation and see plain examples of how we are to proceed. The particular questions we want to answer are: whether or not Yah planned for a man to have more than one wife and, what are some of the things Yah uses to instruct us concerning the Divine Marriage He has instituted?

First, let's start by examining our physical bodies and their capabilities, relative to fulfilling the aforementioned mandate. A woman can, under normal circumstances, accomplish one gestation period per year, which means that she can conceive and bear only one child in a year. We know that there are exceptions in cases of multiple births or perhaps some other special situations. These however, are the exceptions and not what we want to focus on for our purposes. We instead, want to examine the normal situations because they have established patterns which can instruct.

A man on the other hand, has the physical capability to conceivably have as many children in a year as he has wives. This physical capability difference between men and women seems to indicate that Yah prepared them for different roles relative to fulfilling this particular mandate. In other words, for a woman to "be fruitful and multiply," means possibly having at most, one child a year. For a man it means possibly having several children in the same span of time.

It follows, that if a man is to fulfill this mandate in accordance with Yah's particular plan for him, he requires more than one wife but for the woman to fulfill her's, she only needs one husband. If you doubt this analysis, perhaps you have a better explanation for why men and women were created so differently in this regard.

There are of course, some examples in nature where Yah only intended the male to impregnate one female, as in the case of the drone and queen bee. These are exceptions however, and in this particular case, Yah instituted His own unique measures for ensuring that His will be done. As most know, the queen bee kills the drone after he impregnates her. However, there are far more examples in nature that more closely parallel man's physical marital mandate than the few exceptions that don't.

The fact is that in the vast majority of animal species, especially among mammals, which includes man, we find that the norm is more than one female to one male.

Examples of this are found throughout nature. In the field, there are several cows and one bull; in the pasture, there are several ewes and one ram; in the rain forest, there are several female gorillas and one male gorilla, in the savannah, there are several lionesses and one lion. Or for instance:in the barn yard, there are several hens and one rooster. The list goes on and on. It could be stated that the similarities between man and these other mammals and fowls are purely coincidental and therefore not relevant.

This position however, would be tantamount to denying the intellect of Yah. It would imply that He has no plan and does things haphazardly. As pointed out earlier, when Yah gives us a charge He always provides us a means to carry it out. If Yah hadn't planned for man to

61

have more than one wife and woman to have only one husband, what was His reason for creating us in the manner He did? Why are we designed physically, so similarly to those mammals who were to have more than one female in order to fulfill their mandate?

Let us now note the difference in the birth and death ratio between males and females. In any given period there are at least twice as many female births as there are male births. In addition, males die at a disproportionately higher rate than females. The birth and death ratios alone should raise questions in everyone's mind about whether Yah intended one male to one female.

I assume, that the reader like myself, is well aware that we are not intellectually superior to Yah. Even with our inferior intellect, how many of us would create twice as many females as there are males and then allow a larger percentage of the males to die, if we intended each male to have only one wife and each woman to still have a husband? And we're not even including the other situations, like drugs, homosexuality and jail to which we lose many otherwise marriageable males.

One male to one female is simply not what Yah intended nor what we would intend if we had created the world in the manner Yah did. What possible plan would we have in mind for the other females who would never have a husband simply because of our "bad planning?"

Could we expect social problems to manifest and what would they be? These and other serious questions must be answered by those who attempt to refute the correctness and legitimacy of a man having more than one wife.

"And in that day seven women shall take hold of one man, saying, We will eat our own bread, and wear our own apparel; only let us be called by thy name, to take away our reproach."

Isaiah 4:1

We, unlike our animal counterparts, have greater things to address than simply the physical procreation aspect of our mandate. Our nature is more than physical and therefore in Yah's plan for us He has naturally taken all this into account. For us to stay together we must be equipped with the proper emotional infrastructure to handle Yah's intended marital system.

When we look honestly at ourselves we find that a woman's emotional make-up is such that when she truly loves one man, she's incapable of being in love with another. A man's emotional make-up is different however, and he is capable of truly loving more than one woman at a time.

The Woman And The Price

Due to the corruption and immorality in today's world, a woman may be involved with several men, but she will not be in love with more than one. Neither does the fact that she may be involved with several men indicate that Yah intended for her to do this. We know from several Yah inspired sources that woman was only to have one man and that her violation of this Divine directive costs her dearly.

Some of these Yah-sources reveal their information through our ability to discern while others are passed on through the Holy Scriptures and other inspired writings. Ben Ammi discusses the price women pay for these violations in one of his earlier books:

She has waged war against God and lost. All of the abominations mentioned could have been prevented simply by believing and following God's instructions; but instead she rebelled against Adam and followed the law (instructions) of the devil and made herself an enemy of God. It is no wonder then that today all women are suffering from what is called "female sickness." Disease exists in the female sex organ at a ratio unparalleled in history.

Venereal disease has become so widespread and pandemic, until certain viruses are now being passed on to the young daughters, who have become victims of their mothers' disobedience unto God; subsequently, those in their early and pre-teens are now experiencing "female troubles." Some of these viruses are virtually incurable, and when detected, the women are advised to discontinue childbearing.

A woman's menstruation cycle lasts for seven days starting from the time her blood issue begins. It does not end with the ceasing of her flow, because some women only flow three or four days. (Her body is in menstruation for seven days). When the blood spots are mixed with secretions and man's sperm, they form a deadly acid called "pad" which coats the vagina, cervix and womb thus weakening the tissues.

It was considered to be a danger of such magnitude that even the thought in a man's mind to approach a woman in her issue for sexual intercourse was considered a sin. Why was so much emphasis placed upon forbidding the mixing of blood, sperm and secretions even five thousand years ago? God's way of life is like a shield against evil: without it you are vulnerable to any and everything.

In today's world of rampant promiscuity, literally almost "anything goes." This mentality is exacting a high price on us in terms of deformed bodies and minds.

**God the Black Man and Truth
by Ben Ammi, Communicators Press**

Additionally, the scriptures instruct us not to sow diverse seed together, saying that it is an abomination and therefore any progeny therefrom will likewise be an abomination. This admonition applies to both plants and animals, which include man. When a woman becomes involved with more than one man, she is violating Yah's prohibition, by accepting both physically and spiritually diverse seed, which is an abomination. No such Divine Prohibition exists against man planting his seed in diverse soil. These are not merely interesting points to be taken lightly. A thorough understanding of them is a key determining factor in the success or failure of a marriage.

"Ye shall keep my statutes. Thou shalt not let thy cattle gender with a diverse kind; thou shalt not sow thy field with mixed seed; neither shall a garment mixed of linen and woolen come upon thee."

Leviticus 19:19

"Thou shalt not sow thy vineyard with various seeds, lest the fruit of thy seed which thou hast sown, and the fruit of thy vineyard, be defiled."

Deuteronomy 22:9

Monogamy Breeds Contempt For Yah

If you don't know that a man is supposed to take more than one wife, you will resist any attempts to establish a marital relationship which would include this principle. You will insist on following the dictates of the corrupt monogamous society which taught you it's anti-Yah doctrine. You will fail to see the pattern of suffering produced from that incorrect and unrighteous marital system. Monogamous societies breed dishonesty and frustration into the relationships under their marital system. The men in these societies are forced to deny their real feelings and real activities concerning other women.

Remember, it is the males in these societies who have promoted the wholesale marketing of illicit sex as a major commodity. This is their misguided, frustrated response, to the demand from their society, that they live monogamously. Restrained from legitimately pursuing their mandate from Yah, they have become perverse, creating all kinds of illicit means to satisfy their impulses. Their women are forced to pretend that they don't know that their men are, at the very least, interested in other women, or worse, other men, if not actually involved with them.

Both the woman and the man in these relationships end up living a lie and suffering the mental and emotional consequences of doing so. The alternatives they face are admitting the truth, becoming estranged, getting a divorce and then living with the after effects of a broken home. These are only some of the problems experienced by those living under monogamous systems.

Due to the lack of sufficient men for the amount of women, there is no smooth transition, from the home of the parents to the home of the husband. Therefore, many women end up living on their own and seeking alternative life styles. Since few women are prepared to volunteer for "old maidhood," many become "the other woman" and turn into "home wreckers" in their attempt to secure a man. Some women turn to prostitution and seek to satisfy men who are frustrated by a system, that has virtually castrated them, through the lie they are forced to live. While other women adopt the fabled fox's "sour grapes" philosophy and forsake entirely the pursuit of a legitimate relationship with a man. These women often turn to lesbianism, beastialities and other forms of perversions or "looseness".

It becomes obvious that Yah would not be the author of this confusion. It then also becomes obvious that the pain, jealousy, envy, covetousness, hate, perversion, deception, immorality and so on, which are the outgrowth of monogamy, can only be the products of the spirit of err. Armed with this understanding, we cannot be confused by the adversaries of Yah who constantly attempt to persuade us to abandon Yah's plan for that of satan's.

The often conflicting "opinions" concerning whether a man should be allowed more than one wife, primarily come from western societies. They reject the multiple wife concept, asserting that it is unfair, chauvinistic and immoral while endorsing and allowing all manner of perversions and inequities to proliferate.

Of course, there are instances in polygynous societies where some of their assertions are true and must be condemned wherever they occur. But by the same token, there are scores of instances where women are treated just as badly or worse in these monogamous societies. Such abuse is not only committed by individuals but occurs also on an institutional and governmental level.

68

The number of battered or abused women and those who fall victim to domestic violence, have reached epidemic proportions in America, Europe and throughout the western world, all bastions of monogamy. Women have quite often been denied basic rights in some polygynous societies, but one would be hard pressed to find a monogamous society where women have received equity without a fight. In fact, the women's lib movement was spawned and gained momentum due to the inequities women suffered in monogamous not polygynous countries.

Suffice it to say, that in the world today, the hands of both monogamous and polygynous societies are much too dirty to point fingers at one another. They suffer equally from the same affliction and don't recognize it. Neither one has Yah and the genuine desire to fulfill His will, as the cornerstone of their nation building or institution building process. Instead, they seek to preserve and give legitimacy to the very things that cause all the pain and suffering.

Under the guise of "protecting the rights of personal freedom," many western countries have lowered the age of consent to 11 or 12 so that perverts can legally have sex with children. They contend that these anti-Yah relationships and activities are legitimate and morally correct. These same perversion advocates contend that women who are part of relationships where there are more than one wife, are exploited and treated like chattel.

Interestingly enough however, in the same breath that some of them condemn Yah's order, which provides for more than one wife, they advocate and condone same sex marriages, necrophilia, pedophilia and almost any other kind of perversion as sacrosanct personal freedoms, "not to be tampered with" for any reason.

There is definitely something wrong with a system which says, "You cannot have two wives but you have the inalienable right to copulate with another man or a child or something dead." They advocate these things despite the fact that they are abhorrent to Yah.

"Mortify, therefore, your members which are upon the earth: fornication, uncleanness, inordinate affection, evil desire, and covetousness which is idolatry, For which things sake the wrath of (Yah) cometh on the (sons) of disobedience."

Colossians 3:5-6

"If a man also lie with mankind, as he lieth with a woman, both of them have committed an abomination: they shall surely be put to death; their blood shall be upon them."

Leviticus 20:13

"Know ye not that the unrighteous shall not inherit the kingdom of (Yah)? selves with mankind, nor thieves nor covetous, nor drunkards, nor revilers, nor extortioners, shall inherit the kingdom of (Yah)"

1 Corinthians 6:9-10

Their obvious lack of discernment, sometimes outright evil intent and proclivity toward pushing an evil agenda, renders them totally unfit to even enter discussions concerning things like justice, truth, morality, fairness, right or wrong, etc. We must therefore, discount any assertions coming from these quarters on the subject of what is or isn't correct, relative to relationships and marriage.

We can safely conclude that the ill treatment of women in relationships is not based solely on the type of marital system adopted by a given society. The reality being, that it is now and has always been, due to the lack of Yah in the society and therefore in it's marital relationships. When a society is not governed by Yah, then neither are the relationships that it produces. Instead, everything, including its marital system is governed by the spirit of err/satan.

ONLY A DYSFUNCTIONAL, DISEASED AND CORRUPT MIND WOULD REASON, THAT FOR A MAN TO ENTER ANOTHER MAN'S RECTUM IS MORALLY CORRECT AND THEREFORE ACCEPTABLE AND THEN IN THE SAME BREATH CONDEMN THE MARRIAGE OF MORE THAN ONE WOMAN TO THE SAME MAN, AS ORDAINED BY YAH, AS BEING TOTALLY UNCONSCIONABLE.

KNOW OF A SURETY THAT, the road to hell is easily identifyable because you will always find demons treading upon it. They will oftimes be accompanied by lost souls who, in their attempts to find their way, had the misfortune to ask the wrong traveler for directions. Far too many suffer because they have been misdirected as to where to go and how to get there.

The demon you met on the road convinced you to follow him to hell, by portraying it as heaven and wreaked havock in your life and relationships in the process. Remember, satan has designed his world and death-support-systems to appear one way when in reality, they are something quite different.

Consider and keep in mind these facts :

1. Monogamy is the system of marriage which produced the alarming increased divorce rates of 78% and the equally frightening 35% decline in marriages over the past quarter-century.

2. Western civilizations under "monogamy" have made the embracing of abominations a way of life i.e., homosexuality, pedophilia, necrophilia, lesbianism, etc.

3. A large percentage of women are guaranteed, never to have a husband during their entire lifetime, under the monogamous marital system due to the numerically fewer men than women.

4. Unmarried women comprise the vast majority of the world's prostitutes, lesbians and "home wreckers."

5. Yah ordained that a man should have more than one wife to fulfill the mandate He gave to man and provided the means to make this viable, i.e. more females than males, different reproductive systems for men and women, different emotional make up for men and women.

6. More females than males is the standard throughout the creation with most animals for the same reason that this ratio exists for man.

7. Women were ordained by Yah to have only one man and pay a very dear price, in terms of physical, mental and emotional suffering, for violating this Holy Directive.

73

The Infallibility And Governing Power Of Law

To even hope to achieve sustained harmony, peace, love, joy and happiness in a relationship or any other endeavor, one must come to grips with **"LAW."** Laws are the guidelines of life for a people living under the rule of Yah. First and foremost, we must all realize that everything is governed by law, either the greater law or the lesser law. The greater law governs the things you were meant to do, should do, must do and admonishes you concerning the things that shouldn't be done. It also regulates the blessings and rewards or possible punishments that accompany compliance or violations.

Yah instituted only the greater law which instructed man concerning the things he was to do and how he was to do them. For instance, the greater law gave us the proper diet for longevity and perfect health. A diet fit for the Sons and Daughters of Yah. This law helped us to understand that the original thought of Yah was all positive and did not have a prohibitive aspect except where wrong was concerned.

Some examples of greater laws are:

·Thou shall love the lord thy Yah with all thy heart, soul and might and thy brother as thy self.
·Every herb bearing seed upon the face of the earth and every tree in which is the fruit of a tree yielding seed, to you it shall be for food.
·Plant six years and in the seventh year the land shall have a sabbatical.
·In all thy ways acknowledge Yah and He shall direct thy path.
·Be thy brother's keeper.
·Feed the hungry.
·Help widows and orphans.

These are some of the greater laws and they hold blessings for those who live by them. In the beginning we were given the greater laws and we only did that which was the will of Yah. The lesser laws only came into existence when man turned aside from Yah's ways and sought to validate his right to do things contrary to the will of Yah. At that point, the civil or lesser laws concerning what man can do (in opposition to Yah) began to govern.

Some examples of lesser laws are:

·A child can legally engage in a consensual sex act as long as their partner is within four years of their age.
·It is legal to sell and eat USDA approved meats.
·You may legally worship any god you want including satan.
·A man can legally marry another man or a woman another woman in some states.

The choice is in our hands as to which laws we want to govern us. Each of us on an individual level determines, by our deeds and actions which law and it's resulting effects, will govern our lives. In every aspect of life there are governing laws. There are dietary laws which instruct you concerning what is proper to eat or drink and how and when you are to do this. Following these laws will cause you to be healthy and energetic. Disregarding or violating these laws will cause you to be sick and eventually die. There are laws which govern agriculture, education, brotherhood, child rearing, community development, clothing, government, male/female relations and everthing else.

Laws are also formulas which standardize procedures for accomplishing the things in life we need to do. The reason some farmers have bountiful harvests is because they follow the laws governing farming. Farmers are instructed through the law to plant at certain times of the year. The law provides the correct formula for how much space to allow between each plant and between each row. These Divine Instructions inform the farmer of when to begin weeding and when to do the harvesting. It is because of the law and the farmer adhering to it that the good harvest can be gathered.

It has to be understood that law is not a respector of persons. It does not yield to sentiment, desire, awareness nor your acceptance or rejection. It is not influenced by trends or general consensus. Neither your strengths, nor weaknesses, hopes or prayers, sincerity or hypocrisy can affect or alter the law. It is indeed infallible and therefore must be acknowledged. The consequence of failing to acknowledge law is a lifetime of frustrated efforts, unsuccessful endeavors and deficient relationships.

This is not to imply that Yah cannot or will not extend His mercy, if He sees fit and by so doing, spare us the full brunt of the law's consequences. This however, is the exception when He chooses and not the rule He established. Yah is not enamored of us for repsecting the laws of men while ignoring the laws He has established. Nor is He mollified by our acknowledgement of laws which we have no choice but to observe. For who wouldn't call out and seek Yah when facing personal disaster or death as the alternative. Yah wants you to be lawful of your own volition out of your love for truth.

We have been taught all of our lives to follow rules and obey laws. As children, we were taught to cross the street at the corner and only when the light turned green because this was the law which regulated traffic. By observing this law our lives are protected and we avoid the problems associated with stepping in front of moving vehicles. In school, we were taught that the only way to gain proficiency in addition, subtraction, division, etc. was to learn, practice and apply the governing mathmatical laws to any equation we were attempting to compute.

We were taught to observe the laws of the society in which we lived for our own protection and to be "good law abiding citizens." All of this not withstanding, when it is suggested that the universe is governed by Divine Law which must be observed, problems appear. We are taught in the religious institutions that the laws of Yah are no longer in existence and therefore need not be adhered to. We erroneously believe that, anything which doesn't kill us immediately or cause instant injury, is either alright or the violation doesn't count.

Many spiritual laws are given lip service but too few are given the respect which they should be given. Disregarding them works to the detriment of the individuals involved but has no effect on the laws themselves. A perfect example of this is the widely used cliche "you reap what you sow." The first question would be who, other than farmers, gives any real credence to this spiritual law? More often than not, even the farmers only apply it to their crops.

The next question is, do you get an exemption from the consequences because you choose to disregard this law? The answer is an unequivocal, "No." The fact is that the pain and suffering experienced by most people is a direct result of disregarding laws such as this. Even though people rarely realize it, they become their own worst enemy by disregarding these laws. Of course physical laws which no one can get around are accepted and respected, like the law of gravity.

It is commonly understood that if you step off the roof of a twenty storey building that you will plummet to the ground and be killed, therefore few people are tempted to defy the law of gravity. In like manner, few will disregard the law governing the lungs and the need to take in air and not water.

77

These and many other physical laws will cause you to instantly feel the consequences associated with a violation, therefore most people respect these laws. You must however respect both the overt physical laws as well as the not so apparent spiritual laws.

There are fundamental pieces which must be placed in the puzzle of life and among the first ones to be fitted in, is law. You cannot get around the law, even though you might think you can. Therefore, it is in your best interest to learn about law and get in harmony with it. Knowing and acknowledging that there are laws which govern the relationship is only the first step. This knowledge will however, allow you to pursue a course of discovery which will lead to the nature and essence of those laws being revealed to you. With the acknowledgement that law does exist and that it governs totally, we are ready for the next step.

"Know of a certainty, that blessings come from living your life in accordance with the applicable laws governing the various situations encountered in life. Know also, that curses come from violating the laws that govern the situations encountered in life."

Your relationship is governed by law, therefore, without even knowing you, I can state without equivocation that if you are having problems in your marriage, either you, your spouse or both of you (which is most likely the case) are violating or have violated Yah's laws which govern relationships. I can predict with certainty that, if you are not having problems now, you will have them later, if you are not living your life and conducting your relationship in accordance with laws.

What does this mean in practical every day terms? How can I prevent new problems from developing or resolve existing ones? How do I turn my relationship and marriage around?

How do I get myself and my marriage in harmony with these laws? Let's take things relative to law step by step.

Step 1: Understanding That Law Exists

As stated before, your relationship like everything else is governed by laws. There are some laws which relate to men and others that relate to women and there are those that relate to both. You should know as much as possible about laws from each category because those from the categories that govern you must be adhered to by you. Knowing about the laws from categories that relate to your spouse, can provide vital understanding with which you can help your spouse to better adhere to laws governing him or her.

Step 2: Getting And Staying On Your Square, Accepting and Committing To Law

Recognition that law exists and governs is important, but it only becomes beneficial if it leads you to accept and commit to following it. You would be suprised at how many instances there are where things are acknowledged as being correct or even crucial but are none-the-less disregarded. We can certainly attest to the fact, that there are very few people who don't recognize and acknowledge the dangers of smoking, yet the cigarette industry continues to boom.

Mere recognition and acknowledgement is not enough. You must proceed on to the point where you are committed to living in accordance with the laws, whose existence and relevancy you've acknowledged.

Committing to this will require a change that cannot be compromised, because if your commitment can be compromised, the spirit of err will enter in and cause you to lose any ground you might have gained. Your change will have to be capable of withstanding the inevitable onslaught of temptation, doubts, insecurities, anger, fear, frustrations and other torments. All of these elements will arise to challenge your faith in the path you've chosen.

One of the better illustrations of this point can be seen in the story of King David and King Saul. When David was still a shepherd boy tending his father's sheep, Yah sent His prophet Samuel to anoint him King of Israel. After David was anointed, it took 14 years before he was able to claim his rightful place as king because the former king, Saul, was not obliged to abdicate the throne.

Saul attempted to kill David continuously and had him hunted day and night. David had to live as a fugitive in constant fear for his life as a result of Saul and his evil campaign against him. During the years in which Saul illegally occupied David's throne and hunted and tried to kill him, David had several opportunities to kill Saul. Killing Saul would have solved all of David's problems. He certainly would have been justified in doing so, given all of Saul's provocations.

The law, however, stated that you should not touch Yah's anointed. Saul was anointed by Yah, therefore David was bound by the law, not to avenge himself on Saul. His commitment to the laws of Yah was such, that despite the situation, he had to remain on his square and not harm Saul. When a soldier eventually killed Saul at Saul's own request, David had him executed for violating this law.

His uncompromising stand, to remain within the realms of the law, eventually won him a kingdom and the everlasting love of Yah. In fact, he was referred to as the "apple of Yah's eye" and Yah promised that in the last days His kingdom would be established in the house of David. The lesson to remember here is simple; the laws of Yah are to be observed no matter how difficult, but the rewards are truly great. Taking a position like David's will place you on a road that initially may seem difficult to travel, but believe me, it's well worth the effort. Your efforts will be rewarded with achieving the kind of marriage, you and your spouse came together to create in the first place. And besides, since it's **the law,** nothing else will work anyway.

The changes you make as a result of your commitment to "living lawfully," is what I refer to as "getting and staying on your square." Imagine if you will, that every part of your life is comprised of individual squares. There would be a square representing your work and everything related to it. There would be another square representing your civic or national responsibilities, and yet another representing your marriage. For every area of life there would be a square. Within these squares would be all of the guidelines, and laws, etc. that would govern that particular aspect of your life.

Living a lawful life under your mandate from Yah, will require that you always stay within the parameters of your square. Which is simply observing the laws relative to each aspect of your life. A commitment to lawfulness is a commitment to doing things in your life according to the instructions of Yah. Here, we are specifically discussing your commitment to staying on your square relative to your marital relationship. It will ultimately be necessary to get on and remain on all your squares to achieve total oneness with Yah. For now however, we want to remain focused in the areas relating to our subject.

Step 3: Which Laws Must I Observe?

When this question enters your mind you should already be at the point where you have decided that Yah's way is your way. If you are waiting to find out what the laws are before you commit, forget about it, Yah doesn't work that way. He won't accept you as a conditional adherent. You can't make deals with Yah which in effect say, "If I like or agree with a particular law I will follow it." The blessings you are seeking won't come to you if that's your attitude.

Your commitment must be to conform to Yah's directives whether you agree with all of them or not. If by chance you happen to disagree with one, **you must quickly do all in your power to resolve the problem within yourself so that you can be in agreement with Yah. Remember that it is you and your marriage which are out of cycle with Yah and in need of His blessings and not He who is out of cycle with you and in need of yours.**

Yah does not expect each and every person on earth to be able to recite verbatim, each law He has established. This is especially true in today's world where the things of Yah have been relegated to a one day a week religious vanity trip. He does however, require that each of us pursue an understanding concerning Him and how He would have us live our lives. When we actively seek the things He has determined for us, He will provide us with the understanding we need.

Your pursuit thus far has lead you to a point where Yah is providing you with some of what you need, through this book. I say this because you should understand that Yah will reveal His truths to you through a variety of means and you must be ready to receive His word however it comes. Yah has said, " Seek ye first the Kingdom and all things will be added to you." This is more than true when attempting to gain knowledge about His laws and which ones govern which subjects, etc.

We are particularly blessed in this dispensation to be able to have these questions answered for us. Yah has provided us with several means through which we can receive an understanding of His word. These include, but are not limited to, The Kingdom of Yah and it's Holy Leadership, The Re-established Prophetic Priesthood, The Holy Writings, Sons and Daughters of Yah, and the gift of discernment. By accessing any of these or other Holy Sources we can obtain the answers to any law related questions.

"And I say unto you, ask, and it shall be given you; seek, and ye shall find; knock, and it shall be opened unto you. For everyone that asketh receiveth; and he that seeketh findeth; and to him that knocketh it shall be answered"

Luke 11:9-10

The Scriptures explain that the woman is to be a helpmate to man and is to reverence and obey him. This represents the basic law governing her in the relationship. The man is instructed to love her as he loves himself, maintain her in the ways of Yah, and to provide and protect her. Aside from his greater responsibilities to Yah, these are the laws that govern him in the relationship. From these basic laws, each of them can determine what they should or shouldn't do in their marriage. From the following examples we can see how this works.

The law which established woman as a helpmate to her lord is a part of her square that clearly shows how she is to conduct herself in a number of day to day situations. She cannot refuse to prepare his meals or maintain his clothes or look after his children, etc. and not be in violation of the law requiring her to be a helpmate. In whatever area he needs her assistance, she is required to comply if she is to fulfill this particular law.

She cannot be disrespectful to him and at the same time observe the law stipulating that she should reverence him. Nor can she disregard his instructions without violating the law

83

requiring her obedience. There are a host of laws by which she is to govern herself in the marriage. Each must become a part of her, if she is to be happy and fulfilled.

He, on the other hand, cannot be abusive or unfair and be in compliance with the law requiring him to protect her. He cannot deny her the things she is rightfully due and not violate the law which says he must provide for her. Nor can he treat her unjustly or in a mean or evil manner and be in harmony with his mandate to love her as himself. The laws which govern man and give him his instructions and responsibilities are also the source of his authority. Violating these laws and his responsibilities, negates his authority in the relationship.

These are only a few of the basic laws governing men and women in their marital relationship but you can see how they set the tone for the marriage. There are of course other laws that Yah has established to govern particular relationship issues which you will have to learn. However, if you are prepared to apply the laws we just discussed as well as righteous reasoning and humility, you will have a strong foundation on which to establish or re-establish a relationship.

A marriage that is seriously ailing can be restored to health if the parties involved are willing to apply these laws and principles. In the event that you are the only one in your marriage willing to make these changes, **make them anyway.** In many situations, it only takes one person, moving in the correct direction to influence the others to also want to change. A big plus for you is that once you become a lawful person, Yah and all of the righteous forces in the universe come to your aid. The impact on your marriage will be dramatic and your life will improve.

As stated previously, law governs everything! You must remember this at all times, even in your darkest hour. When you truly understand this, you have the power to redirect everything in your life back onto the proper path by simply becoming lawful yourself. Therein lies your protection from harm and your guarantee of success. Please, use your head and think. Can you fill a glass with water simply by holding it under the tap? The answer is "no," you must first turn on the faucet. Prior to doing this, you will not fill the glass. It is the law governing the use of tap water.

No matter how hard you pray, or how thirsty you might be, or how sincere you are in your desire for water or how deserving you might be because you have always given water to the thirsty; unless you observe the law and turn on the tap you won't fill the glass. Your marriage will only be correct if you conduct yourself correctly regarding the laws governing marriage. These laws will support you when you're right or condemn you when you're wrong; your gender doesn't matter.

The law will not allow an unrighteous, unlawful man to rule over and tyrannize a righteous, lawful Daughter of Yah. Nor will it permit an unrighteous, unlawful woman to torment or hold hostage a righteous, lawful Son of Yah. Either the transgressor will be changed or the transgressor will be removed.

Things you must understand about "LAW"

1. **That laws govern everything in the creation including relationships and marriages.**

2. **That the success or failure of your relationship or marriage hinges upon how well you and your mate observe and function relative to relevant laws.**

3. **You, as an individual, must learn about and commit yourself to observing the laws that**

are pertinent to you and you must encourage your mate to do the same.

4. You cannot allow adversity, anger, disappointment, envy, pride, ignorance or any other negative influence to induce you to abandon your square.

5. Know that there are laws that govern men and other laws that govern women but that there are also laws that govern both men and women and they all must be observed.

6. Know that Yah is not pleased by you observing the laws of men while ignoring His laws.

7. Yah is not mollified by your merely observing those physical laws that will bring about your immediate destruction if you violate them, such as the law of gravity or the laws governing breathing under water, etc. while you disregard His spiritual laws.

8. It is gross stupidity to expect a blessed relationship or marriage if you are not conducting your life in accordance and in harmony with the laws of Yah that govern the receiving of blessings.

Chapter 3
Stage 1
Divine Preparation

The Perfect Paradigm

When thinking of life and all its possibilities, most are hard pressed to seriously consider anything as having the potential to be perfect. We are constantly encouraged by naysayers to not expect perfection. By expounding such phrases as "nobody's perfect" or "in all good there is some bad" or "what goes up must come down", "we all have to die from something" and on and on and on, we become convinced that no real perfection is possible. Unfortunately, this intrinsic pessimism tends to impact negatively on our real efforts to achieve perfection and thus, becomes a self fulfilling prophecy.

We must know and believe that reaching perfection is possible before we can possibly achieve it.

In the marshal art of karate, one is taught to break bricks and thick wooden boards with their foreheads or bare hands. When faced with such a challenge, most people think it impossible to do, or at the very least that they could never do it. This will remain true only as long as they think that this is the case. The students in these classes are taught to **think through the brick or board.**

When students become capable of thinking in this manner, they will strike with enough strength to break through. However, until they achieve this mental mastery, they shouldn't attempt this feat because they will only strike hard enough to break their hand or head. Their own doubt will cause them to lessen the strength of the blow. In a like manner, when we lose the ability to know that perfection is achievable, we lose the ability to achieve it. Conversely, with the true knowledge of Yah, we can once again know that perfection is achievable and how to achieve it.

With regards to our subject, perfection is not only possible but achievable by all who would apply themselves with the required seriousness. **It is not necessary to suffer painful, unrewarding interpersonal relationships when the formula for experiencing Divine Holy Relationships is within our grasp.**

Simply being in a relationship is not what we need or desire. We need Divine Relationships. Divine Relationships are those that are established and maintained in accordance with the guidelines of Yah. As such, they are the only ones capable of attaining the perfection we need, in order to bring the long-lasting joy we desire. What is offered in these pages are essentially two things, one of which fits the needs of everyone seeking a Divine Relationship:

1. The opportunity to understand how to start and maintain a Divine Relationship from the very beginning.

2. How to correct existing relationships that need to become Divine.

The Urgency Of Clarity

The Perfect Paradigm provides the formula by which those who want to create Divine Relationships can do so from the start. With the correct understanding of the components that make up a Divine Relationship you will possess the tools needed to build one. Its important to gain this clarity early on, if your realtionship is to start off right.

To be or not to be ? .... clear!!! That is the question, and also the answer.

All too often, the results we seek turn out other than anticipated due to our lack of clarity concerning the vital issues governing them. By not being clear, we neglect to factor in the seeds of success, while allowing the weeds of failure to proliferate, virtually unhindered. Nowhere is this more negatively felt than in our interpersonal relationships. In many, if not most cases, we go through life totally oblivious of this lack of clarity. Thus, we labor under the misguided belief that the pits into which our relationships fall are caused by simply bad luck, bad people, bad choices or insensitivity on the part of someone else.

Our attempts at solutions therefore, tend to miss the real issues and focus instead on either dissolving the relationship, if we're not married or stoically enduring the pain if we are (for as long as possible).

A little more clarity at some earlier point could have avoided this impasse or the right amount, even at this point, could possibly restore the relationship.

A Divine Relationship like anything else, needs to be approached from a point of understanding. There are questions that should be asked and answered before the start of any relationship, most of which should be asked of oneself. In this way, we gain valuable clarity early, which can guide the development of the relationship in the proper manner.

In The Beginning

As someone develops in the Kingdom of Yah, (The Hebrew Israelite Community) he or she is continually being introduced to new and different concepts. Things like sharing and caring take on new dimensions, so do things like love, respect, brotherhood, sisterhood, family, "personal business" or independence, not to mention Yah, the Bible, the Holy Land, our perception of ourselves and the world around us. We are taught new and better ways to eat, dress, talk, and so on. There is virtually no area in life that's not being redefined and taught from "the Kingdom perspective."

Among the primary things being taught, are those relating to the marital system and how to conduct oneself in developing Divine Relationships. There has been so much discussion on this matter that at this point, just about any adult or even many of the older children in the community can tell you the three basic stages involved in the formation, advancement and consummation of a Divine Relationship. However, even though they know the stages, some still have difficulty defining their true in-depth meanings.

So, despite the availability of this great wealth of information, many still experience difficulties in building the kind of dynamic relationships they desire.

Some don't know what to look for in a potential mate nor what they should be bringing to the table. In other instances, individuals simply do not possess the wisdom or knowledge to adequately fulfill the requirements of either a newly developing relationship or a long standing one. Still others, are unaware that they need clarity or guidance. They believe erroneously, that they are equipped to handle things on their own.

Generally, their misconceptions regarding the true meaning of what is taught, renders them unable to get satisfactory results from their efforts, when attempting to employ the teachings. Additionally, I have also found that quite often, the problem lies in accessing the information, understanding it once obtained, or knowing how to apply it in practical terms. There is however, another problem which crops up on occasion and that is when there is an unwillingness on someone's part to seek solutions because they have become entrenched in negativity due to the effects of their exposure to the disinformation.

If these misconceptions can present obstacles to the proper development of those who are regularly exposed to these great truths, how much more so the vulnerability of those who only have "the lie" to look to for guidance, in their quest to form meaningful and lasting relationships. The primary focus of this writing is to provide insight and direction to those seeking to experience truly Divine Relationships. It is my prayer however, that it will also assist and motivate the unwilling to become willing and the uninformed to become informed.

In this manner everyone can experience the joy Yah intended for us when He created man and woman and the institution of Divine Marriage. Let us now proceed to examine the first stage of a Divine Relationship.

The Preparatory Period

Contrary to what one might assume, Divine Relationships do not begin when a man and a woman acknowledge an attraction for one another. They in fact begin long before this point and in the best case scenarios, years before. Divine Relationships begin in what I call "the preparatory period" or the period of "Divine Preparation."

The preparatory period is a time in which an individual learns and then incorporates Kingdom "isms" or the truths of Yah into his or her being. It is during this period, and through diligent effort that one is reconfigured into a Son or Daughter of Yah. Becoming a true Son or Daughter of Yah is a journey of enlightenment where you throw off the trappings of a world that is based on self and take on the mantle of servitude to Yah. **Recognize that you can only be a son or daughter to a father that you are willing to listen to and be guided by.**

"And he answered them, saying, Who are my mother and my brethren? And he looked around about on those who sat about him, and said, Behold my mother and my brethren! For whosoever shall do the will of (Yah), the same is my brother, and my sister, and mother."

Mark 3:33-35

A key to preparing yourself for a future Divine Relationship is ensuring that your concept of why relationships and marriages exist between men and women and the purpose of Yah are one and the same. All too often, men and women have completely different reasons for coming together than Yah had for bringing them together. The end result of being at cross purposes with Yah, is the epidemic of unfulfilled relationships and failed marriages experienced by many. This like other preparations must be made during this period. These prerequisites will determine if one is to later be a part of a Divine Relationship.

There are four basic issues and their accompanying criteria, according to the plan of Yah, which must be learned and understood during this period, relative to Divine Relationships. You must arrive at the point where you are clear on:

1. **What you must bring to a Divine Relationship in terms of your character and understanding.**

2. **What are your legitimate responsibilities or the things you must do in a relationship?**

3. **What should you look for in a relationship in terms of the character of a potential spouse?**

4. **What should be your legitimate aspirations or what should you expect from a potential spouse?**

After getting a clear understanding of what the above-mentioned points entail, you must then examine yourself to see if you meet the standard. The same standard exists for men and women even though there are different particulars for each. The standard is, that both must fulfill their particular mandate from Yah. The particulars are, that men are to comply by doing that which is mandated to man and women are to comply according to that which is mandated to woman.

Under the Preferred Order of Yah, men and women can know of assurity their perspective roles. This empowers them to determine the kind of relationship they are going to have because they will understand what they should orshould not do or expect. In other words, simply comply with Yah's instructions!

The Man: How To Comply

"Let us hear the conclusion of the whole matter: Fear (Yah), and keep His commandments; for this is the whole duty of man".

Ecclesiastes 12:13

The Preferred Order of Yah instructs man to hold fast to the hand of Yah, for woman to hold fast to the hand of man, and for children to hold fast to the hands of their parents. What does this mean as a mandate for man? Into what does this translate when it must be acted out? How does it fit into the Divine Relationship? The answers require man to submit and look to Yah for the guidance and direction he needs in his life. He is to seek to be in compliance with all laws, statutes and commandments. Man is to totally submit to the Divine Will of Yah so that everything he says or does is a reflection of what Yah would have him to do.

"Submit, yourselves, therefore, to (Yah). Resist the devil, and he will flee from you."

James 4:7

By keeping his hand in the hand of Yah, man will be refashioned in the image and likeness of Yah to become a Son of Yah. As such, he will walk in Yah's ways, he will guide his family onto Yah's path, he will support and enforce Yah's ordinances and always protect and care for Yah's creation. This son will be sensitive, loving and responsible in the handling of his wives, children, and the affairs of his family and nation.

Though he will be firm when required, he will never be abusive, cruel, vindictive or begrudging and will continually seek the Yah solution to any situation. This son will function with the understanding, that comporting himself in this manner is required if he is to fulfill his mandate and be pleasing unto Yah. These same personality characteristics and behavior patterns will be brought to any relationship into which he enters, thus making him appealing and desirable as a husband/lord.

"As obedient children, not fashioning yourselves according to the former lusts in your ignorance. But, as he who hath called you is holy, so be ye holy in all manner of life. Because it is written, be ye holy; for I am holy"

1 Peter 1:14-16

"…and it shall come to pass that, in the place where it was said unto them, Ye are not my people, there it shall be said unto them, Ye are the sons of the living (Yah)."

Hosea 1:10

As a son of Yah, man is mandated to guide all things in the creation in such a manner as to keep it in the Divine Cycles established by Yah. His conduct and adherence to the principles of truth is therefore critical. He cannot command, in the name of Yah, that everything and everyone function accoding to its proper cycle if he himself is not in compliance with Yah's cycle for him.

A Divine Woman will find in him the qualities and attributes which will inspire her to love and trust him enough to submit to his lordship and place her life in his hands. In complying with his mandate, he will attain the moral footing to seek and expect to receive, a likewise compliant Divine Woman.

The Woman: How To Comply

The Preferred Order of Yah instructs man to hold fast to the hand of Yah, for woman to hold fast to the hand of man, and for children to hold fast to the hands of their parents. What does this mean as a mandate for woman? Into what does this translate when it must be acted out? How does it fit into the Divine Relationship?

A woman must be willing to look to her Divine Man, who is her lord, for the guidance and direction she needs in her life. She must seek to be in compliance with all laws, statutes and commandments especially those that govern her specifically. She must be willing to totally submit to the Divine Will of Yah (represented by her lord) so that everything she says or does is a reflection of what her lord (or Yah) would have her to do or say.

"Wives, submit yourselves unto your own husbands, as unto the Lord. For the husband is the head of the wife, even as (The Anointed) is the head of the (congregation); and he is the savior of the body."

Ephesians 5:22-23

By keeping her hand in the hand of her lord, the woman will be refashioned in the image and likeness of her lord, to become the Daughter of Yah, for which she was destined. As such, she will walk in Yah's ways, she will help guide her family along Yah's path, she will support her lord in the enforcement of Yah's ordinances and the protection and care of Yah's creation. This daughter will be sensitive, loving and responsible in handling the affairs of her lord, family and nation.

She will never be disrespectful to her lord, disobedient, abusive, vindictive, jealous or begrudging and will continually seek the

Yah solution to any situation. This daughter will function with the understanding, that comporting herself in this manner is the only way she can fulfill her mandate from Yah or be pleasing unto her lord. Finally, she must entertain no doubts that this is the only way she will ever realize the love, peace, joy, harmony and fulfillment she seeks in life. This same conduct and willing personality characteristics will be brought into any relationship she enters, thus making her appealing and desirable as a wife.

"And Adam said, This is now bone of my bones, and flesh of my flesh; she shall be called Woman, because she was taken out of Man."

Genesis 2:23

A Divine Man will find in her the qualities and attributes which will inspire him to trust and love her enough to accept her as a wife and take responsibility for her life into his hands. By fulfilling her mandate, she will attain the moral footing to become a part of a likewise compliant Divine Man.

"Who can find a virtuous woman? For her price is far above rubies..."

Proverbs 31:10-31

As stated earlier, the first stage of Divine Marriage or the process of gaining the correct spiritual position and understanding begins long before a man and a women meet. However, gaining it is a very important prerequisite to a true Divine Relationship. Achieving this understanding is in fact so important, that if it's not accomplished beforehand, you will inevitably have to return for it at some later point in the relationship, in order to iron out problems that were created because you neglected it in the first place.

WHAT YOU PUT INTO PREPARING YOURSELF FOR A DIVINE RELATIONSHIP IS OF PARAMOUNT IMPORTANCE. BECAUSE IT WILL DETERMINE YOUR "DIVINE APPEAL" AND NOT LEAVE YOU BANKING ON MERELY "SEX APPEAL".

There are things that both men and women can and should do in preparation for that inevitable day when they will meet someone that will be right for them. In anticipation of that day, make sure that these things are in place:

1. Incorporate the things of Yah into your being.

2. Know what your mandate is, as a Son or Daughter of Yah.

3. Humble yourself and submit to the will of Yah.

4. Reject the teachings of this world and embrace the true word of Yah.

5. Know what to bring to a Divine Relationship, according to Yah's requirements.

6. Know what your legitimate expectations should be, in a Divine Relationship.

7. Be committed to right and only develop a relationship with someone who is likewise committed to right.

Though truly recognized as part of everyday life in the Hebrew Community, this first stage, as herein defined, is not generally acknowledged as part of its official marital system. However, the overwhelming benefits of having this foundation, makes it a "must" for all who desire a Holy and Divine Relationship. We are now prepared to move to the next stage, Divine Pursuit.

101

Chapter 4
Stage Two
Divine Pursuit

What is Divine Pursuit

This will of necessity, be a somewhat involved chapter since it actually introduces the formal structure of the Hebrew Israelite Community's Marital System. This system is important to all people because it, like all institutions established by this community, is Divine in nature and represents the example of how truly Yah inspired people are to fashion their institutions to please Yah.

It is now time for all who seek harmony with the Creator, the end of suffering and the blessings of a Divine Relationship, to embrace truth and reject the lie. The ability to do this is tied to your willingness to chose those infrastructural processes that emanate from the instructions of Yah over those that come from the anti-Yah source. You must, above all, get this understanding!

When asked the question, "What is "Divine Pursuit?" The most common answers, even among those who are suppose to understand are, "This is the period when a man and a woman take the time to determine if they are compatible, can love each other and have the potential for a lasting relationship," or "This is a period of courtship during which, the participants attempt to woo each other into their personal camps."

These and similar responses, for the most part, reflect the old world paradigm, which is generally referred to as, "going together" (if you're from the hood) or "dating exclusively" (if you're not). Clearly, both dating and Divine Pursuit have certain commonalities, which account for the confusion. However, it is the differences between them that are truly relevant and when these differences are clearly enunciated, the confusion is quickly and permanently dispelled.

These differences not only define what each thing is but also determine the "success or failure potential" being built into any relationship developing under its auspices. They regulate what goes on in the mind of the participants, how they view or evaluate one another as well as the relationship itself. Key components are directly impacted by these differences such as, what we believe we should expect or give in a relationship. The failure potential increases tremendously when one thinks they are involved in Divine Pursuit when instead they are, merely dating.

When asked, "Who is the pursuer and who is the pursuee?" one general answer is, the one with the greater or initial interest is the pursuer and the other is therefore the pursuee.

Another frequent response is, that they jointly share the roles of pursuer and pursuee equally. A vast majority answer by saying, that only he pursues her. Finally, there are those who contend, that only she pursues him.

There is also the question of how does one engage in Divine Pursuit? What does one do or not do? To these questions, many varying answers are likewise forthcoming. Some believe that the method consists of the man bringing flowers, taking the woman to movies or on walks and the woman preparing him special dishes and other treats or maybe picking out special clothing or making something for him. While these kinds of things are a part of the process, they are only a small part. These kind of answers reflect the commonalities between the paradigms.

All in all, most can't explain the true nature of Divine Pursuit and have a host of differing concepts about even its superficial aspects. It follows, that if you don't know for certain what something is, you can't possibly participate in it properly. On the other hand, their answers hit home consistently when asked to define "dating". In fact, the definitions most often offered for Divine Pursuit, fit more closely that of "dating".

The true and correct answers to all of the questions can only be found in the proper definition of the terms themselves. The dictionary definition for dating refers to an action or actions geared toward wooing someone by going to parties, movies or other places of entertainment with them. Also, spending time with someone to develop a romantic relationship. There are no references to Yah in the definition of dating. Primarily, the man pursues the woman because she is considered the prize. Also according to the dictionary, the word pursuit refers to; the chase, hunt, search, or quest; and the word Divine refers to something Godly, heavenly, righteous or spiritually correct.

In short therefore, Divine Pursuit is defined as: a godly quest; a righteous search; or a heavenly hunt, for a proper mate. Ostensibly, these definitions would appear to give us the required clarity regarding both terms, which it does, relative to the term "dating" but not "Divine Pursuit." It falls short of the mark in defining Divine Pursuit because it doesn't take into consideration the intentions of Yah, the author of the concept, and the whole Divine Pursuit cycle. This cycle requires that the Preferred Order of Yah form the foundation and govern the relationship.

Armed with only the understanding gained from simply knowing the dictionary meanings for these words, one will not know to factor the Preferred Order of Yah into the definition nor, will they receive an understanding of what that order is. This causes a gross misunderstanding to take place at the very core of one's perception of what a relationship should be. Yah's preferred order has to be at the root of the definition in order to establish the parameters from which true understanding must come.

When we lack real knowledge of how Yah defines things, we operate in ways which neutralize even the best of our efforts. **By laboring under a false understanding and not knowing Yah's definition of Divine Pursuit, we unwittingly destroy or seriously hamper our chances for a Divine Marriage at this very early stage of the developing relationship.**

Under Yah's order, man is instructed to pursue Yah and woman is instructed to pursue man. This is not simply some chauvinistic exercise in male dominance, but a very important component in the creation process. Originally, man was created in the image and likeness of Yah and was given dominion. He was also given instructions on how to keep all things in harmony with Yah and His Divine cycles.

Man was instructed to always pursue Yah. By man's words and deeds, he was to seek to convince and constantly assure Yah that he wanted to be under His rulership and guidance, and that he was forever poised to be molded and shaped by Yah. Man was to show in every way that he wanted Yah to chart the path he was to walk. In total humility, he was to demonstrate continually, that he fully accepted that Yah was the potter and he was the clay.

His acceptance of this Divine Order in his relationship with Yah assured him of his place as Yah's representative in the creation, with dominion over all things and the continued blessings of Yah. Only when he ceased to think and function in this manner, did he fall from grace and forfeit his position and his blessings. However, in his returning to this position, all that was lost is now being regained.

"And (Yah) said, Let us make man in our image, after our likeness; and let them have dominion over the fish of the sea, and over the fowl of the air, and over the cattle, and over all the earth, and over every creeping thing that creepeth upon the earth."

Genesis 1:26

To this regenerated man must come a regenerated woman. She is instructed to pursue this man in the same fashion that he must pursue Yah. In so doing, she will then receive all of the blessings to which taking her rightful place entitles her. She must realize that receiving the very desires of her heart is dependent upon her accepting that she must pursue the man of Yah and her correct understanding of what that entails.

"And the Lord (Yah) said, It is not good that the man should be alone; I will make him an 'help' fit for him."

Genesis 2:18

"And the rib, which the Lord (Yah) had taken from man, made he a woman, and brought her unto the man. And Adam said, This is now bone of my bones, and flesh of my flesh; she shall be called Woman..."

Genesis 2:22-23

Divine Pursuit therefore, is not merely a man or a woman attempting to gain someone's love and affection by doing things traditionally accepted as pronouncements of love. Instead, a Divine Pursuit can only be conducted by someone who is prepared to say in both words and deeds, "I want to come under your dominion, to be formed and fashioned in your image and to become a reflection of you."

With the correct definition of "Divine Pursuit", coming straight from Yah, it is easy to understand why a man cannot pursue a woman and why the woman must pursue the man. For, how can a Son of Yah say to a woman "accept me under your dominion and lordship, mold me and fashion me in your image?" He can only say these things or take this position relative to Yah, while a woman can and must take this position relative to a Son of Yah if she is to ever be totally fulfilled in a relationship.

Equally important, this understanding provides us with valuable criteria for self-preparation as well as assessing any potential mate. The woman can know beyond a doubt what she should do and how she must approach a Divine Pursuit. She will also know what to really look for in a man and not be swayed by anything superficial. What woman in her right mind will want to say to a man who is not in pursuit of Yah and is pursuing foolish things, "I want to come under your rulership and guidance. Show me the path on which I should walk, mold me and fashion me in your image." If she does, then it would be obvious to anyone that there is no soundness in her.

An American comedian once said, while speaking disparagingly about himself, "I wouldn't stoop so low as to join a club that would have me as a member." So should even a foolish man that possesses an iota of sense feel, toward a woman that would want him to lead her when he exhibits an obviously foolish or un-Yah like nature. By having the correct understanding of Divine Pursuit alone, she will know how to answer the two principle questions of: " What should I bring to a relationship?" and "What should I legitimately expect to find in a relationship?"

Conversely, a man will, as a result of having this definition, be able to know what his legitimate responsibilities are in a relationship and what to look for relative to a woman who is interested in him. Common sense (which, in todays world can only accurately be termed Rare Sense) will tell him that a woman who was truly interested in a Divine Relationship with him would not be fighting his attempts to teach her or guide her.

The woman who was attempting to convince him that she wanted to come under his rulership would not be disrespectful of his wishes or disregard the things he admonished her to do. He will have such a clear picture of what a woman who is interested in him should and/or shouldn't be about that he will easily be able to determine if this is someone he wants to accept as a wife and be responsible for.

I cannot over emphasize how important it is to know how Yah has defined "Divine Pursuit" and to use this definition as the yardstick for measuring yourself and anyone in whom you might become interested. Remember, if you have not prepared yourself correctly for entering into Divine Pursuit or you have accepted someone who is not themselves properly prepared, your relationship is doomed to be anything but Divine.

DIVINE PURSUIT CAN ONLY OCCUR WHEN YOU ARE OPERATING UNDER THE AUSPICES OF YAH, ANYTHING ELSE IS SIMPLY DATING. IF YOU ARE MERELY DATING, YOU CANNOT REALISTICALLY EXPECT TO RECEiVE THE BLESSING OF A DIVINE RELATIONSHIP FROM YAH.

Holy Conduct Begets Holy Rewards

When men and women are involved in Divine Pursuit, they must always keep foremost in their minds, that it is Yah and not the other person, that will ensure their happiness. We must keep our conduct well within the guidelines He has established because His laws govern all things. This being the case, the way you conduct yourselves, that is, staying within the framework of the law or not, is going to have a direct effect on the success or failure of the relationship.

While in Divine Pursuit, pre-marital sex is not to be engaged in nor any other intense activities that can lead to sex. By adhering to this law, children will not be born out of wedlock, with its ensuing social trauma and a whole host of other problems are avoided. The far-reaching consequences of not adhering to this statute have been chronicled throughout the annals of time and need not be elaborated upon here.

"But fornication, and all uncleanness, or covetousness, let it not be once named among you as becometh saints;"

Ephesians 5:3

Usually, in a developing relationship, either both elect to remain in harmony with the law or both agree to violate, especially, regarding the laws governing sexual conduct, since it generally "takes two to tango." However, this unified front is difficult to maintain when adversity strikes, and it does with alarming frequency from the moment your activities take you from under the protection of Yah. Your violation of Divine Laws make you vulnerable to all manner of temptations, irrational thoughts and actions.

Most couples don't realize that it is their joint misbehavior earlier that causes the strife later in their relationships. They

111

fail to link their disregard for Yah in one area with their escalating problems in another. To operate outside of the parameters of the order is in effect, to work against the best interest of any relationship and this is not restricted to sexual misconduct alone. It refers to any violation of any statute of Yah.

"For whosoever shall keep the whole law, and yet offend in one point, he is guilty of all. For he that said, Do not commit adultery, said also, Do not kill. Now if thou commit no adultery, yet if thou kill, thou art become a transgressor of the law."

James 2:10-11

The man who eventually marries a woman with whom he previously conducted an improper relationship, discovers later that his wife doesn't trust him with other women because of what he did with her. She knows from first hand experience that he is no respecter of the law.

When he later tries to correct his wife for an infraction here or there, he is met with an attitude which says in effect: "How can you act so high and mighty and tell me not to violate this or that particular law when you and I violated so many laws together?" As a result of their joint disregard of the law prior to their marriage, this man has virtually given his wife a license to do wrong and therefore both he and she will suffer the consequences.

Likewise, if the wife later attempts to reign in the disorderly, irresponsible husband, she will find that in his eyes, she has no right to expect any other kind of behavior from him. This is because before marriage, she was a willing participant in his disrespectful activities and flaunting of the law. While there are a number of cases where this kind of situation exists, there is one in particular that stands out as an example of how improper conduct comes back to haunt a relationship.

"CJ" was a youngster who from his early school days displayed a proclivity towards rebelliousness and disrespect of order. He was continuously getting into trouble of all kinds. As he became older and his mind began to focus on girls, he was soon in trouble with them. He ran away a few times and once took a willing young girl with him.

"Sis" was about 16 at the time and obviously thought "CJ" was the last word in manhood. They went back and forth a few times and eventually she became pregnant. After the equivalent of a shotgun wedding, they settled down to a life of marital bliss. By the time she was pregnant with her third child, he had gotten another girl pregnant and was no closer to accepting responsibility than he was when they first started their improper activities.

At this point however, "Sis" was ready to settle down and take care of the family. She wanted him to become responsible and conduct himself like a true father and husband. His attitude was still "NO WAY" am I going to conform.

Today "Sis" has three children for which she must be responsible and "CJ" continues to skip merrily along, violating the order of Yah and helping to make "Sis's" life as miserable as possible. He has no idea that there is a real need for change and thinks "Sis" is simply "no fun any more" and "is always nagging."

They argue, fight, separate, get back together, argue, fight, separate, get back together, only to repeat this vicious cycle over and over again as though they were trapped - in the twilight zone. They find themselves continuously at odds with one another and are unable to discover what happened to the love they thought they shared.

He wonders: "Why does she always accuse me of infidelity, gripe about everything I do and refuse to listen to anything I tell her?" Meanwhile, she constantly asks herself, "Why is he so insensitive towards me, irresponsible relative to the family's needs and is hardly ever home?"

These kind of things will continue to happen until the relationship, which started off so wonderfully, is totally destroyed. The person who, in the beginning filled you with joy that knew no bounds, now only generates contempt and pain in your soul. While these relationships can sometimes be salvaged, it is not without a heavy price and in many cases they are never repaired. With this glaring example, it is easy to understand why **pre-marital sex is prohibited during Divine Pursuit.**

On the other hand, the couples that remain in harmony with the order of Yah, continue to rise in love. When situations come up after they are married, they will be able to look to Yah and the law for solutions, comfort and guidance.

The order which they have respected and upheld, will in these times of need, uphold and support them. The wife will be able to trust her husband because she will have seen first hand that he truly stands for the principles he purports to represent. She'll know that he is not weak in the face of temptation nor easily swayed. She will be more than willing to submit to his leadership because he will be a living example of one who reflects and submits to the will of Yah.

The husband will feel confident that he has a wife who is truly a Yah-sent partner in whom he can trust. He can rest in the knowlege that she will conduct herself properly and that if something should be done that's out of order, it will not be viewed as an occurence due to evil intent, but a genuine mistake. An excellent family which typifies the blessings inherent to respect of the law, is the case of Mr. G and Ms. P.

> Mr. G is a man who has pursued Yah diligently since he first discovered the Kingdom. He has been a hard worker who has continously demonstrated his commitment to the service of Yah and his people for many years. As a single man, Mr. G was involved in several pursuits with some great women. He always conducted himself in a manner pleasing to Yah and there was never even a hint that he was anything but upright and spiritually in tune with Yah.

> As we know, Yah is a rewarder of those who diligently seek him and Mr. G's case was no exception. While serving his people on foreign assignment in America, Yah blessed him to meet and subsequently rise in love with the beautiful and likewise morally upright Ms. P.

After a truly Divine Pursuit and Mecodeshet they entered into a truly Divine and Holy marriage and are today, the proud parents of two lovely children, whom they both love and cherish.

Yah and the order which they have upheld, now supplies the support and undergirding they need to build a life of harmony and love. If they remain true to this course and situations do occur, there will always be somewhere for them to turn. All of the righteous forces in the universe will be at their beck and call, for right will be on their side. Mr. G and Ms. P are true examples of how

"Holy Conduct Beget Holy Rewards"

By remaining on this path, their mutual trust in the integrity of one another will continue to uphold them and strengthen their confidence in the Divinity of their relationship. Instead of doubt and recriminations, they will experience greater love and harmony, both with Yah and one another.

What Is My Commitment?

An important point to note about Divine Pursuit is that it is not a period in which a couple is to set up a pseudo or defacto marriage. Instead both retain their status as unattached individuals. Their relationship is therefore informal and not binding. Neither person is required to perform any marital functions or assume those kind of responsibilities. The commitment during this period is to investigate the possibilities for an everlasting relationship. Additionally, to demonstrate your righteous attributes through your words, deeds and respect for the order of Yah.

Neither the man nor the woman should evaluate the relationship based on whether or not the other is doing things, that should rightfully be reserved for after the marriage. However, participants in a Divine Pursuit don't always know what is required of them or what they should or shouldn't require. They sometimes harbor inappropriate expectations. In some instances, not only are the expectations incorrect, but often, there is confusion about what are one's own responsibilities.

An extreme example of this is when a man or a woman feels that they are suppose to provide for the sexual needs or desires of one another when in Divine Pursuit. Nothing could be further from the truth. You should neither expect nor require sex, nor feel responsible to provide it during Divine Pursuit. As stated earlier, not only is premarital sex not required, it is expressly forbidden.

"For this is the will of (Yah), even your sanctification, that ye should abstain from fornication;"

I Thessalonians 4:3

117

Less extreme examples are when a woman is required or feels obligated to prepare his meals or wash and iron his clothes, etc. Just as sex is not a requirement, neither are these kinds of things. There will be occasions when it is perfectly acceptable for a woman to do some of these things for him, however, she is not responsible for maintaining them, as a wife would be. Likewise, he can help her through a financial situation, build a shelf in her room or move heavy boxes for her, etc. He is not to take on the responsibility of furnishing her apartment, paying her rent or assuming financial responsibility for her. He can certainly be there for her but not to the same degree as a lord.

When a man already has one or more wives, this is a good time to begin developing their relationship with the pursuing woman as well. Additionally, if, during this period, either the man or the woman happens to become interested in someone else, they are free to explore that possibility. It may not be viewed favorably by some men if the women pursuing them opt to do this. Their primary thoughts being, she can only marry one man and he doesn't want to risk losing to the competition or if she's really interested in me why look elsewhere?

These are myths! Men, you should remember that no one else can get a woman that's truly for you, so if she does marry someone else, it means that she was simply not for you. The fact is that you are better off finding this out now, before you get married than X amount of time down the road, after you're unsatisfactually married. Another point to consider is the woman who takes her time in making a final determination. There are some who think that women who seem to have difficulty deciding who to marry, and pursues first one man and then another, are therefore fickle.

While this may indeed be factual in some instances, I beg to disagree with the generalization. A woman opting to look at all possibilities is not acting improperly. She has both the right and responsibility to carefully explore all options to best ensure that her final choice is the correct one for her.

We must remain cognizant of the fact that, Divine Marriage is forever, and a woman should know beyond a reasonable doubt that the man she marries is the right one for her. Women are therefore encouraged to be as sure as possible and remember this adage, "If the doubts are strong
enough to make you feel too uncomfortable to decide to go with it........ **Don't.**"

On the other hand, women who don't approve of the man they are pursuing entertaining other interests are admonished to reconsider their opposition because men are in a completely
different position. But just like women or perhaps moreso, men should be as certain as possible when choosing a wife.(We will go more into this in the section on Divine Marriage). However, even though a man can have several wives or be pursued by more than one woman, he can only marry one woman at a time.

Additionally, a pursuit with one woman need not necessarily impact on another pursuit because each woman can conceivably marry the man. This then becomes an early test of whether or not a woman is still operating under the old paradigm or has made the transition into the new. Because the governing factors in the new paradigm are based on the principles of Yah, the things women ordinarily fear are no longer relevant and therefore she can feel secure even when another woman is present.

THE PROPER DEFINING OF DIVINE PURSUIT IS CRITICAL, FOR THEREIN LIES THE REAL FOUNDATION OF THE MARRIAGE. In addition to understanding the structure of the marital system of the Kingdom, those who would successfully partake of it must also clearly understand how each aspect of it is defined. Not confusing Divine Pursuit and dating or Divine Mecodeshet and being engaged, is key to this understanding.

As we conclude our discussion on Divine Pursuit, I admonish you to remember and take to heart these points:

1. The Preferred Order of Yah governs all relationships.

2. Divine Pursuit is not "dating" where you simply attempt to win someone's affections and commitment to you.

3. The woman is to convince the man, in the same manner he is to convince Yah, that she wants to come under his lordship and dominion, to be molded in his image for the glory of Yah.

4. Both must understand that it is their righteousness and submission to the plan of Yah that make them appealing to each other.

5. It is their adherence to the order of Yah that will cause Him to bless their relationship and give them the joy and happiness they seek.

6. Binding commitments, requiring the relinquishing of one's "unattached status" are not to take place at this stage of the relationship.

7. "Holy Conduct Truly Begets Holy Rewards"

When the level of certainty and assuredness in the relationship is reached, whereby both parties feel that they have not only the basic prerequisites and potential for a longlasting and Holy Union, but also the love, genuine desire and will to achieve it, the time to move forward into Divine Mecodeshet has arrived.

Chapter 5:
Stage Three
Divine Mecodeshet

I want to remind the reader that the Divine Marital System we are examining in this discourse is that of the Hebrew Israelite Community of Jerusalem. There are some similarities to other systems of marriage but only peripherally and I caution the reader against drawing conclusions about this system based on their understanding of others.

 As we discuss Divine Mecodeshet, the temptation to think of it as an engagement, as in other systems might occur. It is important to understand that they are not the same. Many commonly accepted practices and commitments which exist during an engagement are either prohibited or are simply not a part of Divine Mecodeshet.

An engagement is a binding commitment to marry someone. This commitment is so binding that there have been many instances where a person has been sued for "breach of promise" when they ended an engagement. Divine Mecodeshet is not a binding marital promise but only a commitment to look into the relationship on an exclusive and serious basis. It is also a time for preparing yourselves for a possible marriage.

Many couples that are engaged, live together like husband and wife. They do everthing that a married couple does and have all the responsibilities to the other person that a spouse would have. The only exception being, that their relationship does not have the legal status of a marriage. An engagement has no requirement for official status and can be entered into by the individual couple without the benefit of a priest or any authoritative body. None of these practices are permitted, required or engaged in during Divine Mecodeshet.

The Holy Institution

Divine Mecodeshet is the stage at which a developing relationship becomes officially recognized. Prior to this, the individuals involved are simply contemplating possibilities. Within the Hebrew Community, this Holy State is initiated by the couple in question formally applying to the priesthood to be placed in Divine Mecodeshet. Once this is approved and the couple is placed in Divine Mecodeshet, an announcement is then made to the community at large, informing everyone of the couple's new status.

As opposed to Divine Pursuit, which was a private decision involving only the man, the woman and their families, Divine Mecodeshet is officially sponsored and community supported. The guidelines governing this aspect of the marital process require that not only the couple comply with certain stipulations but also the rest of the community. For a period of not less than 70 days, this man and woman are to undergo a process designed to identify and resolve any issues that may potentially hamper the forward progress of their relationship.

During this period, they will have a minimum of 10 sittings or counseling sessions with the priest. The priest will teach and instruct them concerning the laws, statutes and ordinances, which are to govern their lives and relationship. The priest will seek to ensure the couple's spiritual compatability as well as their proper understanding of Divine Marriage. In addition to the sittings with the priest, the woman will become more intensely involved with the man's family and any wives he might already have.

More quality time will be spent learning about and restructuring the expanding family. There will be planning sessions in which the priest, the couple and other family members will participate. They will discuss living arrangements, logistical and financial needs, as well as all other aspects of how the family will function, once the marriage has taken place.

The couple in Mecodeshet, is "set aside" to allow special time and attention for one another. This means that there can be no other pursuit for either of them. Unlike the Divine Pursuit stage, where they could remain free to develop other relationships, at this phase, pursuing other "potential interests" is forbidden. This is a time for them to probe deeply into their hearts, souls and minds concerning this relationship, without interference from would be suitors.

The concentrated, exclusive time prescribed during this period is important to both the man and the woman as well as any wives or family he might already have. Divine Mecodeshet is a time for a serious reality check. This is another point that cannot be over emphasized. At this stage, you must know what you are doing. Serious problems that sometimes plague marriages later, are due to things that were not worked out during Mecodeshet.

Since this is the last stage before an eternally binding union is formed, it is very important that couples deal with this level-headedly. You cannot be frivolous in regards to handling this stage of the relationship and expect a problem free marriage. Anything other than total honesty concerning yourself, your intended spouse, the real condition of the relationship, other wives and family, your love, dedication and commitment to the other person and the relationship as well as their love, dedication and commitment to you and the relationship, would be considered frivolous at this juncture.

Quite often when people feel they are "in love" they become very impractical. They cease to critically analyze things and close a blind eye to short comings and obvious character flaws in their **"beloved."**

Such practices are very dangerous because **"what you see, or in these cases, what you don't see, is what you get"**. Acting like an ostrich and sticking your head in the sand will not make something distasteful about your intended go away. You must instead, confront the disagreeable issues and seek to get them corrected.

One of the real benefits of Divine Mecodeshet is that it provides a mechanism which allows you to look more closely at the person that you are considering marrying. Then, if there are things that require change, this same mechanism will help in bringing about those changes. There are those who foolishly say to themselves, when they encounter serious problems in their relationship, "Once we get married he (or she) will change and things will be better."

This kind of thinking is the equivalent to deliberately swallowing a lethal dose of poison and hoping that your stomach fluids will dilute it to the point that it won't kill you. **DON'T DELUDE YOURSELF, YOUR STOMACH FLUIDS ARE NOT THAT STRONG.** If your intended spouse is not motivated enough, by the prospect of marrying you to change, when marrying you is their objective, what will be their incentive after they've accomplished their objective? I remember a case that graphically demonstrates a situation like this.

> "MC" was part of a mission in West Africa, when he was reassigned to America to assist in completing a major project. While there, he met and became involved with "Lady Luv." Their love for one another continued to develop as they moved through Divine
> Pursuit and on to Divine Mecodeshet. About six months prior to the proposed wedding date "Lady Luv" was sent to the West African

mission where "MC" had been serving before going to America. She remained there for the six months until "MC" arrived for the marriage.

Those who were serving on that mission got to know "Lady Luv" during her six month stay and became aware of serious character flaws in her. When "MC" returned to the mission, he was asked if he truly knew this woman. His reply was that he knew she had some problems but they weren't very serious and that they could work them out.

He was told that the best thing for them was to postpone the wedding until these things could be put in order. The counselors advised this couple to have more extended sessions to set them in the proper cycles, which would give them a better chance of success in their marriage.

Both refused to see the truth and would have rebelled if they were not permitted to marry. Despite everything said and all advice to the contrary, "MC" and "Lady Luv" were married on a Wednesday afternoon. They experienced total marital bliss ... for all of nine hours.

About twelve oclock that night, some of the leadership were summoned to the honeymoon cottage. Standing outside, we met a weeping bride who, in a fit of uncontrolled rage had thrown the wedding cake and other nuptial dishes and paraphernalia at the groom.

He then proceeded to eject her from their honeymoon suite, stating that he had made a mistake and wanted out of the marriage.

At this point, those in leadership simply opened the door, gently guided the bride back into the sleeping chamber and closed the door. They left the couple to sort things out, with the admonishment that they had made their bed and would have to lie in it. This union lasted less than a year before the wife ran off to points unknown.

Divine Mecodeshet is the period when you prepare to relinquish your "unattached individual" status. In doing this, you have to be willing to live with your decision forever. You are choosing a lifetime mate which makes this one of the most important decisions you will ever make. In addition to feeling genuine love for the person with whom you are considering sharing the rest of your life, you must feel that he or she is an upright person who desires and is striving to serve Yah. Being sure of these points is very important, but not the only things you need to consider.

You must now look at what I refer to as the
    "Practical Considerations."

129

Putting The Practical Considerations In Place

What I define as the "practical considerations" are all the important and seemingly not so important things that make up your life. This includes: the type of foods you like to eat; the way you think men or women should dress; your hobbies; the things you like to do; the way you like to entertain guests; your work, finances, education, your household dynamics; are you a stickler about neatness; how you feel about studying, excercise, parties, music, books; your position in the hierarchy of whatever organization, group, community or club of which you might be a part, your spiritual and moral position, political views and so on.

These and hundreds of other things make up the practical considerations. I want to take a moment to explain why I refer to these things as practical considerations and why they are so important. Before I go into that however, it is important to note the two catagories into which the practical considerations fall. The first is personal and relates to private preferences, needs desires,etc. The other is public and relates to your requirements based on your interactions with the rest of the world.

Within the Hebrew Community, everything and everyone is under constant world scrutiny. This is because the community has taken on the monumental task of ushering in the Kingdom of Yah. This increases the public aspect of everyone's life considerably. It is therefore a very good example of a prime practical consideration with which they must contend. To address this issue, community members want to make sure that any spouse choosen is committed to living a life that reflects Yah. Only such a spouse can complement them in their ongoing quest to serve Yah.

In order to maintain the proper example for the world, each person within the community must achieve harmony in their personal life and with Yah. It is therefore imperative that potential spouses know and understand the role they are to play in assisting their mates in achieving and maintaining this harmony. Practical considerations impact on the things that effect how one feels and therefore how one acts. They are not however, entirely personal, because their effect will ultimately impact on the community or the world in which you live and are therefore often very public.

Since these things have a profound effect but are different from the emotional aspects of the relationship, I have dubbed them the "practical considerations". Both men and women have practical considerations that need to be addressed, or at the very least, about which an understanding needs to be reached. These things can cause love and appreciation to grow or diminish, depending on how they are handled.

(Naturally, we are not entertaining any possibilities that someone is seeking to have wicked or unrighteous practical considerations, considered.) If you are involved with someone who has wickedness or unrighteousness as part of their akcnowledged agenda, the best thing you can do for yourself is to get uninvolved as quickly as possible.

These things aside, in most instances, the minor practical considerations do little more than irritate when they are not addressed immediately. However, they should be addressed and resolved because they can grow in importance with time. Having said this, we are now free to examine the practical considerations that are often not so minor and do require our serious attention.

Both men and women have to learn about their sexual opposite. There are any number of general things concerning the opposite sex, about which knowing or not knowing could prove pivotal in many situations we face. Getting to a point where you understand most of these general things about the opposite sex is however, only half the battle. You must also decipher how this information relates to your intended spouse in particular.

A major practical consideration of many men for example, deals with taking things that are happening in their homes out side the home for discussion or resolution. Their feelings about this issue range from being totally against it, to welcoming and encouraging it, and everything in between. For instance, in one category there are men who feel that, for their women to go outside the home seeking answers they can't or won't provide, is tantamount to treason at the highest level.

They feel betrayed by such actions, that their manhood is being challenged or that their wives don't trust their judgement. Quite often these men will feel that their wives have become adversaries who are trying to undermine them.

Another category of men will always encourage their wives to seek creditable outside assistance whenever a problem of any magnitude occurs. They feel that getting help is the best way to keep things from getting out of hand. A man from this school of thought will sometimes find himself at odds with his wife if she is more inclined to try and keep personal issues private.

He may question his wife's motives or think that she doesn't want help from others because she is afraid that her shortcomings will be revealed. These represent the two extremes relative to this particular issue and there are a number of different variations in between taken by some men.

Within the Hebrew Community, most men feel that an issue can be taken outside when necessary, but only after they have exhausted their personal resources without successfully resolving the problem. Still others agree with this position but feel that their wives would have to inform them before going to an outside source. This is an example of an important practical consideration that could have serious consequences, based on how it's handled.

When a woman does not know where her intended spouse is on such an issue, she could wind up on the opposite end of the spectrum, suffering the resulting conflicts. Feelings that are very close to the heart must be looked into by both people in the relationship to determine what the real options are. This is one of the purposes of Divine Mecodeshet. To provide a mechanism for dealing with these issues before you relinquish your "unattached individual" status and get married.

Frank discussions must take place relative to how each person feels about issues that often cause conflict between men and women. Only through this type of concerted effort, can one gain an understanding of their intended's practical considerations or convey information concerning their own. It should be noted here that this same criteria can also be used by readers who are not members of the community in Dimona.

Those readers who are a part of or are contemplating becoming a part of a conventional relationship, need to have a period of intense examination of themselves, their partner and the relationship in order to better assess its real success potential. Utilizing this example, let's walk through a scenario which illustrates what to do and how this period can be used to help an aspiring relationship.

First of all, when you get this close to marriage, most of the basic things should have already been covered. Knowing that this is your last opportunity before marriage, to enhance the relationship's success potential and reduce its failure potential, should motivate you to the highest levels of seriousness. You must come out of any intoxicatingly "romantic fog" in which you may be floating and soberly face the realities of your relationship. If the person in whom you're interested has strong feelings about certain things that don't coincide with your own, what do you do?

How do you properly address their practical considerations? Do you seek to appease them? Do you demand that they change? The answers to these questions have to be based on what you can or cannot live with in a harmonious manner. Let's take for instance, the man who doesn't want his wife going outside of the home seeking answers under any circumstances. This can present a very serious problem between the two of them if situations come up that they can't handle.

These problems can be greatly exacerbated if the woman feels strongly that utilizing outside sources should be an integral part of the conflict resolution process. If the feelings of each are so deep that a workable compromise cannot be reached, one of them will inevitably give in, and in effect say: "Ok I can live with us doing this your way instead of mine." Of course, saying this and living with this are two different things and that difference will have to be thoroughly considered before taking this position. To merely acquiesce in order to get married is the wrong thing to do because you will have to live with your decision forever or until the position of your spouse changes.

If you can actually live with this and not regret it later, this could be the solution to the problem. However, imagine what life will become if you can't live with this and change is a long time coming or doesn't come at all. What will be your option then?

Will you still feel that just being married is enough? **I DON'T THINK SO**, in fact it almost never is.

What usually happens is that, if the man acquiesces, he will later become more and more bitter and resentful each time his wife seeks outside assistance. Though, he may try to live up to his commitment, and allow her to seek outside assistance, it will become increasingly more difficult for him to accept. He may reach a point where he is tempted to outright forbid her from continuing this practice, despite his previous agreement to allow it.

Sometimes, due to the fact that he has previously agreed, he will attempt oblique moves to discourage her without blatantly breaking his word. He will become less attentive or speak to her in a sharper manner, if at all. In other words, express a general displeasure with her whenever they interact.

In the event it was the wife who acquiesced, she will feel later, when she wants to get the outside assistance she had agreed not to seek, that she is living under a tyrant with no where to turn and that a vital element of personal choice has been denied her. Because she doesn't have the same direct authority in the relationship as the husband, she cannot simply demand that things be changed based on her new position.

She will therefore, become moody and difficult to communicate with or aloof and distant. She will sometimes develop headaches in bed to punish her husband sexually. Her approach will, in most cases, remain subtle but her displeasure will definitely be felt. Any of these approaches however, will cause strife in the marriage. This situation could have been avoided, if only he or she had been more honest about what they could or could not live with, prior to the marriage.

Another area of concern is work. What you do is most definitely a practical consideration, especially if you have a skilled trade, artistic talent, political position or a profession. Generally, when a person makes their living in one of these areas, they have put in long years of practice, study or hard work to get where they are. Often their work is enjoyable to them and they love to do it. More often than not, when someone enjoys their work and the pay is good, they will put a lot into maintaining or furthering their career in that arena.

This will sometimes place heavy demands on the person's time, attention and energies but because they find it rewarding they have no problem acceding to these demands. This automatically reduces the amount of time, attention and energy they will have for their spouse or family. An individual such as this needs a mate who can understand and support his or her occupational choice and not be in competition with it.

Since this is such an important aspect of life, spouses who are not in harmony in this area almost universally end up at each other's throats. A good example of this is when a woman meets and becomes interested in a policeman. She soon learns (if she doesn't already know) that this person's work is dangerous, time consuming, physically, mentally and emotionally taxing and is truly life threatening.

Based on these things, he will require certain things of any woman he marries. He must assess whether or not she has the mental and emotional make up to properly cope with the requirements of his profession. She must make the same assessment, to determine for herself if she can cope with these requirements. If she can live with and support him in his profession and not become a thorn in his side because of it, this important practical consideration will be in place.

It cannot be a situation where she marries him and later decides that she doesn't like him doing the work he does and won't support him in his chosen career because it's dangerous, time consuming or life threatening. To overlook these important practical considerations is to subject the marriage and yourselves to much unnecessary duress.

The same principle applies when it is the woman who has a career that her man needs to consider. The circumstances may be different but this is still a prime practical consideration. While a woman's first obligation is to her lord and home, she should be free to engage in her other occupational interests as long as they do not supersede her primary responsibilities.

There is a case that comes to mind where the man and his wife needed to deal with this kind of issue and didn't.

> Mr. X was a hard worker and dedicated to the principles of Yah. He was both skilled with his hands and an accomplished athlete. He attempted to keep all of his affairs in order and always took care of his responsibilities and his family. He was married to Mrs. Y, a creative sister who was also good with her hands. She could cook, crochet, sew and do many other things which made her a valuable asset to her husband and family.
>
> After many years of marriage and several children, he met and came to love Ms. Z. Within a short time they began a Divine Pursuit, followed by Divine Mecodeshet and then entered into Divine Marriage. This appeared to have all the hallmarks of a match made in heaven, or at least that's what the participants thought.

137

And maybe it could have been, had they covered all the bases relative to the practical considerations.

Ms. Z was very outgoing, she always had her hand in many diverse activities. She was a mover within the sisterhood and was always involved with public relations. She possessed superb administrative and management skills and loved to do work in these fields. As a result, her expertise was always sought after and she responded to these appeals enthusiastically.

Mr. X was somewhat insecure when it came to his new wife demonstrating such self reliance (or in his mind independence) coupled with the confidence to move out into the world and take charge of situations she encountered. He felt left out and of less importance in her life. This had never arisen as a problem with his first wife.

Mrs. Y had no serious activities or work requirements outside of the home and the small circle in which Mr. X revolved. He therefore, always felt firmly in control and an integral part of everything in which she was involved.

Even before the marriage, Ms. Z had noticed that Mr. X did not show enthusiasm or support for her involvements. He seemed sort of distant or uninterested whenever she would talk about her work.

When he did talk about it or acknowledge it, he seemed to do so in a disparaging manner. He would joke about her being "too independent" and "career oriented." She dismissed this as just his way of poking fun at her.

After they were married however, his jokes turned serious and he began to voice opposition to projects on which she was working. He began to say that she was only doing these things to get away from responsibilities in the home. It seemed as though no matter how hard she tried to balance her household duties, with the kind of work she loved to do in other areas, he was still displeased.

This situation continued unabated for many years and spilled over into every area of their lives, permanently tainting their marriage. The resulting effect was that they experienced an ever increasing strain in their relationship. In the beginning they each had strong feelings about this issue but never reached an understanding of what the real issue was. All they knew was that they were unable to restore the love and joy they once felt.

She resented him and what she considered his insensitivity towards her and everything that meant anything to her. He resented her and what he called, her independent attitude, which in his opinion, violated the very foundation of marriage.

Their marriage continued to disintergrate and after fifteen years they no longer remembered how or why they had become so estranged from one another. The effects were none-the-less just as devastating and eventually this estrangement brought about the dissolution of their marriage.

This is an example where two basically good people striving to remain in harmony with the cycles of Yah, are unable to overcome adversity. The reason being, they failed to examine their developing relationship in realistic terms. Both Mr. X and Ms. Z saw things that clearly indicated trouble up the road but both ignored the signs. Ms. Z failed to ask herself, "Can I live with him and his attitude towards what I love to do?" She did not honestly assess her ability to adjust or the viability of expecting him to change.

Therefore, something that was at first only mildly disturbing eventually became the proverbial straw that broke the camel's back. Mr. X failed to face the fact that he could not cope with such an assertive woman. He knew that he would not be appeased by anything short of her complete abandonment of that aspect of her nature. However, his desire to enter into the marriage made him decide to let it go and deal with it later. He never saw his position as a shortcoming that he needed to overcome and continued to bolster that position with imagined justifications. So the end result was easily predictable.

This could, and does happen quite often in relationships when couples allow "being in love" to blind them to the real facts about their relationship. Again I say, **"Open your eyes and your nose to see as well as smell, the roses."**

"Know that you can live with the person you choose to marry"

For many women and some men, there is a tendency to succumb to environmental pressures to get married. There is peer pressure. "All of my friends are married with families. I must get married to somebody." There is time pressure. "I am getting older and should be married to somebody now." There are family, social, political, financial and a host of other pressures to get married, and do it now.

Thus, one might be tempted to take a deep breath, toss caution to the wind and take the plunge, for all the wrong reasons. Sometimes simply to avoid the embarrassment of having yet another relationship end in something other than marriage, will motivate some to go ahead with a marriage, of which they are uncertain. None of these are acceptable reasons for a pursuit to culminate in marriage, and if you are so inclined, I advise, you to take a second deep breath and **"don't do it."**

You may notice that throughout this book, I continuously refer to definitions to establish the basis for points that are being discussed. It is very important to do this because the way a thing is defined determines everything concerning it. You must be capable of properly defining everything in your life if you are to deal with it correctly. In developing a Divine Relationship, it is Yah's definitions of everything that you must possess. Once you have Yah's definitions, you can proceed to build your relationship correctly, in accordance with those definitions.

Understanding About A Lord

At this juncture of Divine Mecodeshet there is a final hurdle to cross. It requires returning to the correct understanding of "lord." This is a very important and supremely critical matter.
"This is so critical in fact, that if you do not understand about the lord, or don't agree with the designation lord or if you are not prepared to deal with it in its entirety, then based on this single issue alone, I will state in no uncertain terms that, YOU SHOULD NOT GET MARRIED!!!"

Men before you get married and become a **"lord"** you must:

1. Be completely cognizant of what it means to be a lord and commit yourself to those responsibilities.

2. Know that the woman you are marrying understands what having a lord entails and is truly ready for a lord.

3. Be certain that she is ready for YOU, IN PARTICULAR, to be her lord.

You are about to represent Yah in the life of a woman and any children that may come along. Your responsibility will be to order your lives according to Yah's will. You will have to be capable of conducting yourself in a Yah-like manner, at all times and in all things. Only through this conduct will your family have, in their midst, a living example of what Yah is and what Yah wants from all members of His Divine Family.

You will have to exercise self-control in order to qualify to exert control over the family. You will have to possess wisdom in order to wisely administer the affairs of the family. You will have to be honest, fair, compassionate, loving, generous, sensitive and Yah-fearing in order to instill and maintain these attributes in your family. Your judgement must be just, in order to cause your wife/wives and children to believe in and to have faith in you.

Yah and His infallible law will make you lord, with all the responsibilities and authority incumbent with that position. The law will require that your wife/wives love, respect, obey and reverence you but, **it will be you and how you carry out this mandate that will cause them to be endeared to you and desire to fulfill this law**. Yah will give into your hands not only the lives of those who will comprise your family but their very souls.

This is an awesome responsibility, not something to be taken lightly. You will have to vow a vow unto Yah, that you understand and will carry out this responsibility as He has mandated and He will require it of you. Taking this next step into Divine Marriage, will bind you to fulfill the special mandate of lord, **your soul will be held accountable**.

Women before you get married and become a "**wife,**" you must be certain:

1. **That you understand what a "lord" is and what that represents in the life of a wife**

2. **That you are "ready for a lord" to govern your life.**

3. **That you love, respect, reverence and believe in the particular man you are marrying, to the point where you are ready for him in particular "to become your lord."**

Additionally, you must be cognizant of what is required of you, once you accept a lord.

This is not a conditional undertaking. It is not something you do today and reject tomorrow. Therefore, don't accept it lightly or without having thoroughly investigated and assured yourself that this is definitely for you. Once you marry, you will come under the dominion of your lord; you will become a part of him. No longer will you be an individual nor will he remain an individual, but you will be one. **He, as lord, will be the head of this new body and all of the members will be accountable to him. You will be required by Yah, to be obedient to him, respectful of him and to reverence him.**

Your obedience will not only be required when you agree with his decisions but also when you don't. Your respectful behavior towards him will be required at all times, even when you are very angry with him about something, be it real or imagined. You can never raise your voice at your lord nor speak to him in a tone or manner unbefitting a lord. You will have to seek to be pleasing to him at all times and in all situations. You will be required to humbly accept his directions and guidance. You can never disregard his instructions. You will have to have faith in him and respect his judgement in all matters, even those to which you disagree.

Only when a woman understands that to enter into Divine Marriage is to accept this particular man as her lord, in every possible way and is prepared to conduct herself accordingly, should she be prepared to take the marriage vows unto Yah. As a woman you must remember, that the most important thing you can do to ensure your salvation once you've committed your life to Yah is to likewise commit it to the Son of Yah that's right for you. He shall be your lord from whom you should never turn aside.

Only if you are prepared for something of this magnitude should you go forward, and if you are, then go forward with the blessings of Yah.

Recognize and understand that, if you want to marry someone you must be in harmony with their practical considerations and have come to terms with their short comings. Where there is no harmony relative to these issues, it is better not to marry.

Harmony as being discussed here simply means:

1. I am cognizant of the practical considerations and short comings of the person in whom I'm interested.

2. The person in whom I'm interested is cognizant of my practical considerations and shortcomings.

3. I can live happily with and be supportive of the practical considerations of the person in whom I'm interested.

4. The person in whom I'm interested can live happily with and be supportive of my practical considerations.

5. I am prepared to help the person in whom I'm interested to overcome their shortcomings and/or live with the situation for as long as it takes to accomplish this.

6. The person in whom I'm interested is prepared to help me overcome my shortcomings and/or live with the situation as long as it takes to accomplish this.

7. A vital prerequisite for a Divine Marriage is a thorough understanding of and complete agreement with Yah's directives pertaining to "lords."

8. I, as a man, am well aware of the responsibilities incumbent upon a lord and I'm prepared to undertake these responsibilities and commitments.

9. I, as a woman, understand what it means to have a lord and accept that I must conduct myself as such at all times and not only when I agree.

10. I and the person in whom I'm interested, have honestly and seriously looked into our relationship from every conceivable position, and we have determined that we are in tune and in harmony both with Yah and one another and are ready to proceed into Divine Marriage.

Once you and your intended have successfully gone through the aforementioned stages of Divine Preparation, Divine Pursuit and Divine Mecodeshet, you are ready for Divine Marriage. The term "successfully" as applied here, does not mean that you've merely complied with some stipulated time and procedure requirements. Instead, it indicates that the spirit and substance of each stage have been thoroughly ingested, understood and is committed to by the couple. They are therefore true candidates for Divine Marriage.

Chapter 6
Stage Four
Divine Marriage

The Holy Union

Divine Marriage is the Holy State of matrimony ordained by Yah to unite His sons and daughters to bring forth the future caretakers of His creation. This Holy Union provides a base from which the Children of Yah can draw sustenance and support, as they go forth to fulfill their mandate from Him.

A Divine Marriage is a haven in which the righteousness of Yah is embodied. It forms the nucleus of the family and is a microcosm of the community, the nation, the world and the entire creation of Yah. With the Divine Marriage in cycle, the tone is set for the whole of the creation to be placed in the proper cycles of Yah. It is therefore the ultimate expression of the Divine Cycles and order of Yah.

The serious nature of this institution requires that those who would enter into it, have a Yah-like spirit, great understanding and an unquestionable love for one another. You must also be willing to forego the personal, when required and apply nationalistic standards to the goals and aspirations set for the family.

Unlike societies, where men and women marry for any number of reasons, including everything from lust to convenience, from infatuation to acquiring wealth, prominence or political advantage. Divine Marriage instead commits the participants to a life of servitude to Yah. **The primary reason for marriage is to carry out the instructions of Yah and for the perpetuation of His cycles.** Though most societies and people have forgotten this, it remains, the primary reason for Marriage.

Yah intended for the union between men and women to be a Holy Affair, Divinely inspired and perpetually moving forward. The order He set things in was designed to accomplish this result. There were to be no pre-nupitual agreements, no divorces nor other forms of separation once the marriage was established. The Divine Marraige is based on this design and is therefore the only way to achieve the true results marriage was created to manifest.

"... For this cause shall a man leave father and mother, and shall cleave to his wife, and they (two) shall be one flesh? Wherefore, they are no more (two), but one flesh. What, therefore, (Yah) hath joined together, let no man put asunder."

Matthew 19:5-6

What Is My Commitment?

Divine Marriage represents the total lifetime binding commitment of those involved. They are hereafter, as inextricably bound to one another and the laws governing this union, as the members are to the body. You now become truly one and must take vows which attest to your understanding and commitment to this union. These vows are made before both man and Yah and must be upheld by all who take them.

"When thou shalt vow a vow unto the Lord thy (Yah), thou shalt not be slack to pay it; for the Lord thy (Yah) will surely require it of thee, and it would be sin in thee. But if thou shalt forbear to vow, it shall be no sin in thee."

Deuteronomy 23:21-22

The consummation of a Divine Marriage, means that your "individual status", is now happily relinquished. In exchange, you take your pre-ordained position on Yah's winning team, "The Divine Family." Your role in it is clearly defined and your happiness is assured with your compliance. As we have continued to witness, the perfection of Yah is such that everything we are to do has its own built in rewards, and likewise Divine Marriage bears this out. While we seek to carry out the roles Yah established for us, He fills our lives with love, happiness and joy.

"For the woman who hath an husband is bound by the law to her husband as long as he liveth; but if the husband be dead, she is loosed from the law of her husband. So, then if , while her husband liveth, she shall be called an adulteress; but if her husband be dead, she is free from that law, so that she is no adulteress, though she be married to another man."

Romans 7:2-3

"Let the husband render unto the wife her due; and likewise also, the wife unto the husband. The wife hath not power of her own body, but the husband and the husband hath not power of his own body, but the wife."

1Corinthians 7:3-4

The Holy Role Of "Divine Lord"

The husband was ordained by Yah to be the lord of the wife. He is to love her as he loves himself and to be reverenced by her. Yah obviously had a Divine Purpose for establishing the husband as lord, instructing him to love his wife, even as he loves himself and for her to reverence him. What are the reasons for these mandates from Yah? Is it possible for man to love someone else with the same inherent intensity that he loves himself? Why is he lord of the woman and what does this mean? Why does Yah instruct her to reverence him?

These could be perplexing questions, the type which would necessitate seeking out the sages to answer had not Yah blessed us with the gift of discernment. When we examine these questions utilizing this gift of discernment, Yah reveals to us the obvious answers. Yah made man in his own image and likeness and gave him dominion over the entire creation. Man was mandated to manage Yah's creation and order all things according to Yah's instructions.

Woman was taken out of man to assist him in performing this charge. The consistency of Yah ensures that he won't give you something to do and not provide a means through which to accomplish it. Likewise, He won't give you a responsibility without the authority to carry it out. Finally, He would not give you an assistant to help you fulfill your mandate and not put you in charge. Yah not only made man lord over the woman He gave him but He made him lord over the entire creation.

Man was given Yah's plan for ensuring that everything in his creation remained in harmony with His Divine Cycles. This meant, that the woman needed to submit to man in order to learn what her role in the creation was to be and how to perform it. Because Yah made man in His own image and likeness, man is qualified to administer the affairs of the whole creation. He is therefore, eminently qualified to handle his own affairs and those of the woman which, incidently, are one and the same. The question of why his lordship over woman therefore, becomes self explanatory.

"For I know him, that he will command his children and his household after him, and they shall keep the way of the Lord, to do righteousness and justice; that the Lord may bring upon Abraham that which he hath spoken of him."

Genesis 18:19

Why she was instructed to reverence the man is also easily understood. Man was to be her teacher of the things Yah intended. He was to guide her on the proper path and be the source of all the things she required in life. Within his mandate as lord, man becomes the link between his wife and Yah. She's required to be humble and reverence him in order to ensure that she will listen to and accept direction from him. In this manner, she could receive the blessings required to sustain her existence.

"For the man is not of the woman, but the woman of the man. Neither was the man created for the woman, but the woman for the man."

1 Corinthians 11:8-9

Yah could be assured that man could love woman as he loved himself because man and woman are one. Man is therefore, loving himself when he loves woman and demonstrating his love for Yah. It is easy to love oneself when you are in harmony with Yah. When the wife is in harmony with her lord, who is in harmony with Yah, he sees himself in her, in the feminine form.

154

He sees the perfect manifestation of the Preferred Order of Yah, thus, he can love her with a perfect love.

His love for woman and for Yah also provides the motivation and inspiration for him to carry out his responsibilities as lord, in the proper manner. The lord is to provide, protect, teach, guide and govern; and he is to do so fairly and justly with compassion and sensitivity. These things can only be done, and in this manner, through love. It goes against the grain to mistreat or be unfair to someone you love. Even the most wicked, seek the best interest of those they love; how much more so, the righteous?

"Husbands, love your wives, even as (The Anointed) also loved the (called out assembly), and gave himself for it, so ought men to love their wives as their own bodies. He that loveth his wife loveth himself. Nevertheless, let every one of you in particular so love his wife even as himself; and the wife, see that she reverence her husband."

Ephesians 5:25, 28, 33

The Holy Role of Divine Wife

Yah determined, that the man He had created could perform His assigned duties in the creation only if he had the necessary assistance. To provide this much needed assistance, Yah created the woman from the rib of man and referred to her as a "help fit for man." The instructions given to her was to submit herself to man, to obey, love and reverence him. The Divine Wife is to allow herself to be molded and fashioned in the Yah-like image of her lord. She is to be his right hand and chief assistant.

Woman was never to seek to be liberated from man, any more than he was to seek to be liberated from Yah. She was to seek greater and greater oneness with man. Yah never intended woman to pursue a separate agenda from that of the man. He did not create her to conflict with man or compete with him for dominance. The Divine Wife is a complement to man, a Holy extension of him. It is through the wife that a host of things are accomplished which help man to fulfill his mandate from Yah.

She is a vital part of the survival system Yah designed for man. Her being formed from the rib of man is a prime indicator of her role as protector of man. In the same way that the rest of his ribs serve to protect his vital inner bodily organs, so was the rib which became woman was to protect his vital outer bodily organs. The inner bodily organs protected by the rib cage are the heart, lungs, liver, spleen, etc. The outer organs of man which are to be protected by the "rib/woman" include: his household, children, harmony, health, diet, reputation, well being, etc.

The wife is the one who is to receive and nurture man's seed and bring forth his children. This as we all know is Yah's way of perpetuating life. This function is of unparalleled importance in the creation scheme, for without it, the creation would cease to exist and man would become extinct.

Her role after conception is equally important because she is to nourish, nurture and rear the young child in accordance with the laws and statutes of Yah. Additionally, she is to teach the child in the ways of Yah and ensure that discipline and order are indelibly imprinted in his mind and spirit.

The order of Yah placed the wife in the role of mother of man's children and maintainer of his home. She performs her functions with diligence and loving concern. She prepares the food which nourishes the family and at the same time teaches the children how to feed themselves. She cleans and orders the household and at the same time teaches her young daughters how to manage and maintain a tidy, well-run home. As she bathes the children she is also teaching them how to properly clean themselves.

A Divine Wife is a living example of what Yah would have all women aspire to become. The manner in which she comports herself demonstrates to young girls and other women their role under Yah's Divine Order. Her relationship with her lord is at all times humble, respectful and loving, illustrating clearly how a woman is to interact with her lord.

"In the same manner, ye wives, be in subjection to your own husbands that, if any obey not the word, they also may without the word be won by the behavior of the wives, while they behold
your chaste conduct coupled with fear; whose adorning, let it not be that outward adorning of braiding the hair, and of wearing
of gold, or of putting on of apparel, but let it be the hidden man of the heart in that which is not corruptible, even the ornament
of a meek and quiet spirit, which is in the sight of (Yah) of great price.

For after this manner in the old time the holy women also, who trusted in (Yah), adorned themselves, being in subjection unto
their own husbands, Even as Sarah obeyed Abraham, calling him lord; whose daughters ye are, as long as ye do well, and are not afraid with any terror."

1 Peter 3:1-6

"That they may teach the young women to be sober- minded, to love their husbands, to love their children, to be discreet, chaste, keepers at home, good, obedient to their own husbands, that the word of (Yah) be not blasphemed."

Titus 2:4-5

A woman, in accepting man's (her husband, her father, her employer) authority over her, should realize that she is setting a positive example for her children to follow by allowing their father to lead. This does not disqualify her from ever having authority over a male; it merely prevents attempts to supplant man or transform herself.

Thus, when the parents in turn instruct their children to "just say no" to drugs, premarital sex, and other foolishness, the child can draw the required strength from the loving exemplification of his parent's behavior in governing his own behavior.

**God and the Law of Relativity
by Ben Ammi, Communicators Press**

The Divinity of Familyhood

The family which is produced from the Divine Marriage, teaches its members how to serve Yah in every way. It places Yah at the forefront of everything in which the family is involved. The absolute first test anything must pass, if it is to be considered by this family is whether or not it is pleasing to Yah. Does whatever it is fall within the guidelines established by Yah? If so it can be undertaken but if it can't, it has no place with this family.

Together the lord and his wife teach their children to examine, everything they encounter, under this spiritual microscope. Everyday decisions like what to have for dinner or what to wear to school or who should be our friends and associates are measured by this yardstick. This Holy Lifestyle carried out by the Divine Family provides the foundation and the proper environment for developing the upcoming generation into Sons and Daughters of Yah.

In this family the children learn Holiness, by doing all things in a manner pleasing to Yah. They learn to view life and the creation from the correct perspective. These children will grow up and won't experience the relationship related problems that many adults today are forced to face. They will have effortlessly passed through the "Divine Preparation" stage because of the Holy Lifestyle their Divine Family lived, as a result of the Divine Marriage of their parents.

Boys growing up in such an environment will have in their father, an example of what a man should aspire to exemplify in his dealings with everything related to the family. He will learn to be responsible and sensitive in his relationship with his future wife/wives by the living example of how his father conducts himself with his wife/wives.

Because a young son is always aware of what his mother is feeling, her happiness with his father will motivate him to replicate his father's conduct in the future when he begins to develop relationships.

He won't be prone to involving himself with gangs or other anti social behavior because he will feel secure and self confident due to his family life. He will have no need to try to establish his manhood through the methods of the streets. His later attraction to the opposite sex will not merely be based on harmonal activities but also on true respect and appreciation of the finer qualities that Daughters of Yah are endowed with or work to aquire. He will require more than just sex in any relationship he forms. He will have seen first hand the benefits of proper involvement with a Divine Woman because his mother will be one and his father will have demonstrated his appreciation of her virtues.

A girl from such a family will not be insecure like many women because she will know that a strong family with a strong Yah minded man at the helm will form a solid foundation for her and her children. She will want to remain virtuous so that she can attract a man of true substance and not have to settle for one who might only have surface or material substance. Likewise she won't be insecure relative to other women because her biological mother and other mothers (her father's other wives) will have demonstrated the beauty and benefits of life with one another and their lord, her father.

As she grows and develops she will be self confident because she will know her own value and worth based on how she has applied the things taught to her by those in her Divine Family. All children's initial experiences in life come from their home and family. It is only later that other outside influences begin to impact in their lives. With a solid Divine Family background, steeped in Yah consciousness, and the continuing back up and support of this strong family unit, these children will be capable of resisting the traps layed out for the unsuspecting.

We live in a world that constantly bombards our children with activities, concepts and negative influences that all but guarantee that they will have major problems in their lives. They are subjected to these influences in school, at play, in books, on the television, on the internet, from relatives and friends, on posters and billboards and many many other diverse sources. It is little wonder that they grow up and have disastrous relationships, marriages and lives.

The Divine Family forms a hedge around them which blocks many of these influences from even reaching the children, as they grow and develop. Those that are impossible to block, (and there are many) are at least filtered through this hedge of truth and cannot present themselves as the final word on anything, therefore allowing the things they learn in their family to maintain hedgemony during this critical period of their lives.

I therefore want you to understand that creating and maintain a Divine Family is one of the greatest gifts parents can give to their children. In fact, it is virtually impossible for them to develop properly without it.

Expanding The Divine Marriage

According to the mandate of Yah, in a Divine Marriage a woman can marry a man who already has one or more wives. Therefore, the day will inevitably come when this will occur in many marriages. How this is done is as important to the outcome, as is the spirit and minds of the persons involved. Taking on additional wives is second in seriousness, only to that of taking on the first wife. Being second is only because they joined the family after the advent of the first wife and not due to any lessening of their importance or position.

When a woman in the Hebrew Community decides she is ready to marry into a family where one or more wives already exist and that family is prepared to accept her into the family, it means that the process described in the preceding pages has been completed. That process was developed to ensure the best possible results in the marriage. Its purpose is to remove all obstacles and create a solid foundation for building a stable marriage. One that will continue to grow and expand as more children are born and more wives are added.

Any time a man marries, whether it is to his first wife or any subsequent wives, he is required to wait a minimum of one year before marrying another woman. Likewise he is not to begin the development of a new relationship during this period. This means that even the informal stage of "walking and talking" prior to Divine Pursuit is prohibited. The purpose of this is to give the newly weds time to effectively meld as husband and wife.

This exclusive time period also gives his other wife or wives and the new bride an opportunity to develop the oneness they need as sister-wives. There is a need to do this without having another developing relationship and its requirements, pulling on their time and energies. During this period, the man

163

will teach his new wife how to fit into his family and life. For most young women who have never been married or involved with a man, this period is crucial in helping them to develop into the wives they are to become. However, even women who have been previously married, need this time to learn how to best mesh with their new lord and family.

"When a man hath taken a new wife, he shall not go out to war, neither shall he be charged with any business: but he shall be free at home one year, and shall cheer up his wife which he hath taken."

Deuteronomy 24:5

The root of monogamy is selfishness, which convinces women that they should not "put up" with another woman. It has even been stated that two women cannot cook in the same kitchen. Yah however, did not structure His world in this fashion. His world was constructed in a manner designed to bring His daughters together and not tear them apart. By marrying and becoming one with a Son of Yah, a woman likewise becomes one with the wife or wives he already has.

There are particular requirements placed on each adult in the marriage, when a new wife becomes a part of the family. The husband is required by Yah to be fair and impartial in his handling of all situations relating to his wives. He cannot, because of his love for one wife, neglect or otherwise discriminate against another. He must adhere to the same set of guidelines relative to new wives, that he was admonished to observe and fulfill when he married his first wife. Additionally, marrying another wife does not diminish a man's husbandly responsibilities towards any wives he may already have.

In maintaining his responsibilities towards his wives, a man is to treat them equitably. Equity is an essential ingredient to

164

have in a Divine Marriage where there is more than one wife. It should be understood that we are talking about equity and not about equality. To the uninformed I say, there is an important difference between the two. This difference must be noted and explained by the lord to his wives if they don't already know the difference. It is everyone's commitment to equity that will help maintain proper balance in the marriage.

Equality, means that everything is done on an even basis or the same thing in the same way for each wife. For instance, if a husband gives one wife flowers he will give each wife flowers. If he takes one to the movies, he will take each of his other wives to a movie. Equity on the other hand, means that each wife is dealt with according to her particular needs and requirements in a loving, fair and just manner.

No Son of Yah is required to deal with his wives in the fashion prescribed by the tenets of equality. Sometimes wives or husbands will expect equality to exist in their marriages. Whenever this is the case, that marriage will suffer unnecessary stress and strain. A husband who feels that everything done for or with one wife must be duplicated with each of his other wives is inviting hardships into his life. In addition to placing himself into an untenable position, since he cannot realistically maintain such a regimen, he is also teaching his wives to have unreasonable and improper expectations.

This kind of thinking inevitably leads to a mentality in some wives, to live by comparison. Therefore, they will judge the value of their lives based on what is occurring with others, rather than what is occurring with them. They will seek to ensure that whatever another wife receives, they also receive and when they don't, they will feel deprived or abused. This mentality will in time, breed jealousy, envy and strife between wives who are taught to expect equality rather than equity.

165

Misunderstandings and improper expectations such as these are automatically precluded, when it is clear to everyone that a Divine Marriage is not a competitive or a comparative undertaking. Instead of simple equality, it is based on equity where one is required to give according to their ability and receive according to their needs and legitimate aspirations. Additionally, when a man accepts another wife, the wife or wives he already has, likewise have also taken another wife and are therefore required to assist in acclimating the new bride.

Their role consists of welcoming her in a loving and sisterly manner, assisting her in learning about her new husband, home and family. They must recognize that she has the same Yah given right to be there as anyone else in the family and should be treated as such.

New brides are to enter their new marriage with the understanding that they are part of a Divine Process, designed to further strengthen and bolster their lord and family in their service to Yah. She must realize and accept the fact that the purpose of her being allowed by Yah to become a part of a Holy and Divine Family was to fulfill His will. Her blessing in this is that, as she strives to fulfill His will, her righteous desires will also be fulfilled. It may not be without trials, but Yah will deliver.

New wives should never think, nor should husbands give the impression, that they are there to "straighten out" the existing wives. Neither should they think, that they are somehow better, more loved or are in a stronger position in the marriage than their sister-wives. They are in no way to contribute to the feelings of insecurity, that may be experienced by some sister-wives. Establishing the best possible relationship with her new sister-wives, lord and family, must be among the highest priorities on the agenda of a new bride.

Often when discussing expanding the Divine Marriage, I will compare a new bride entering a man's family to a new baby coming home for the first time. When a baby is born, he is a little stranger to the family. Some of his siblings may be happy he is there, others may feel threatened by his presence. Each will have their own thoughts about the event but reality will dictate that, each will have to come to grips with the fact that, **"THE BABY IS HERE TO STAY!!!"**

Some are happy and pleased because they see potential in the new relationship. They may think, "now I have a baby brother to play with" or "when he gets older we can go to school together" or a host of other pleasant thoughts. They will be prepared to receive the blessing represented by the advent of the new baby. Meanwhile, another sibling, who was not so pleased by the baby's " invasion of his world," is thinking, " Now my parents won't have time for me" or " I'll probably have to share my toys with him." This sibling will think of reasons not to welcome the new baby.

The parents are of course jubilant over the new arrival. His coming is a blessed event which brings them great joy. As good parents, they will be prepared to help their other children deal with whatever adjustments they need to make. For the siblings who welcome the baby, the parents will teach them how to safely handle the baby. They may teach them how to feed and change him. They will allow them to hold and rock their little brother and so on. To these siblings the new baby will represent a real blessing, from day one.

The other sibling will require a different approach. Due to his insecurity, he will demonstrate his/her displeasure with the new baby and cause the parents to be concerned. Initially, the parents will try to encourage him to develop another attitude about the baby. They will point out good things about the baby and show how he can help his parents take care of the baby, etc.

If this sibling does not change his attitude in a given amount of time, his parents will change their approach. The results will be that this sibling will be denied free access to the baby and at some point bring on the wrath of his parents. At this juncture, a situation which the sibling did not want to develop becomes a reality because of his negative approach to avoiding it.

In a like manner, some women will react unfavorably to a new wife coming into the family. This, like the second sibling might be due to feelings of insecurity, jealousy, envy or just plain old selfishness. In some instances these wives will seek to find reasons to reject the new wife. They will only see the negative of the new bride and be oblivious of her positive characteristics. This, they feel will justify rejecting her. There is this irrational thought somewhere in the back of the subconscious minds, of both the second sibling and his counterpart among the wives that, eventually this unwelcomed person will go away if they refuse to accept their presence.

This wife must also come to grips with the reality that, **"THE NEW BRIDE IS NOW PART OF THE FAMILY AND IS HERE TO STAY."**

Any other position will not be received well by the husband and will lead to a strained relationship between him and the offending wife. He will naturally drift away from the wife who is creating the disharmony. When a woman rejects her sister-wife, she is also rejecting her lord and Yah. Therefore, it's the wife that's doing the rejecting that ultimately ends up rejected. Again we see how employing improper methods to avoid something imagined, can cause your imaginings to become reality.

Women should also understand that having "sister-wives" is a special blessing. Wives who understand this and conduct themselves accordingly, have found someone who can be more than a sister and a friend.

There are many blessings that women receive as a result of having sister-wives that are missing from the lives of other women who are not so fortunate. There are blessings which are so obvious that they should even occur to the minds of people who are from monogamous societies. For instance, there is always someone with whom to share the normal household responsibilities such as cooking, cleaning, sewing, bathing the children and so on. These and a hundred other daily chores are reduced, providing more time to do the things that a wife and mother might not otherwise have time to do.

More importantly, as women move back into the correct cycles of Yah and the observance of His laws and statutes, other needs become apparent. A good example is the laws of purification, specifically regarding a woman's monthly menstruation period. According to the law, a woman is to be separated for seven days during her monthly cycle. She is not to prepare food, sleep with her lord or come into physical contact with him, or anyone else for that matter. She is to be **"inactive,"** to rest and regenerate. By so doing she increases the longevity of her life.

While Daughters of Yah are observing this law each month, their families and lords would need others to come into their home and perform the functions of a mother and wife if there is no sister-wife. With a sister-wife, life in the home is only minimally effected by a wife's monthly cycle. The wife on her cycle is also blessed because she has a sister who loves her and will look after her needs, which allows her the opportunity to get the rest she needs during this period. She receives this blessing one week of every month during her inactivity.

Another purification law instructs that a woman who has had a baby be inactive for a period of eighty days if it was a girl and forty days if it was a boy. One can really appreciate the provision Yah made of a sister-wife, when the time arrives to fulfill this law. The relationship that can develop between Divine Sister-Wives who care for and serve one another is a blessing to behold. These are but some of the reasons that Divine Wives willingly embrace their new wife when she becomes a part of their Divine Family.

Also by demonstrating their willingness to embrace their new sister-wife, they will also show their lord that his agenda is also their agenda, that his submission to Yah's will is humbly emulated by his wives in their submission to his will. As a result, everyone will experience the blessings of having a new wife in the family, instead of the wrath which would develop if the wives, like the other sibling, choose to reject the new wife.

Wives in a Divine Marriage must be clear on the fact that, it is not they, who are sharing "their man" with other women. Instead, they must understand that it is Yah who is sharing "His son" and "His daughters" and therefore "His blessings" with each of them. Additionally, it is important to remember the following:

1. Divine Marriage is the only marital system ordained by Yah and can only exist for those who are willing to humbly submit to His will.

2. The lord is responsible for providing, protecting, teaching and keeping his family in the Divine Cycles of Yah.

3. Wives are to submit to their lord and assist him in fullfilling his mandate from Yah; this is her whole duty.

170

4. The Divine Family is to provide the stable Yah-inspired environment in which the future caretakers of the creation will be formed and fashioned into Sons and Daughters of Yah.

5. Husbands are to accept the responsibility of having more than one wife and function in accordance with Yah's guidelines with regards to this mandate.

6. Wives are to welcome other "sister-wives" and help them to become part of the family in a loving and sisterly way.

7. The whole purpose of this institution is to carry out Yah's Divine Will for His creation and we are rewarded in the process with love, peace, joy and personal fulfillment.

When presenting the marital system of the Hebrew Israelite Community of Jerusalem, I am presenting what I refer to as "The Perfect Paradigm." Having gone to great lengths to explain and demonstrate its viability and achievability, from the beginning of a relationship; we now want to explore how to achieve a Divine Marriage when you are already in a marriage or a relationship that is not so Divine.

CHAPTER 7
Don't Be Your Own Worst Enemy;
Reconfiguring The Less Than Divine

A Divine Reassessment

For many if not most, "The Perfect Paradigm" is something they missed the opportunity to experience, because they didn't begin their relationships as they should have. Within these relationships are all kinds of unproductive excess baggage. This excess baggage was either brought in by both parties at the beginning or picked up along the way. How this excess baggage has accumulated is of minor importance. What is of paramount importance, is the fact, that it must be identified and gotten rid of.

This baggage is all of the false concepts, beliefs, positions, expectations and so on that determine your understanding of what a relationship should be. We need to take a moment to assess where we are pertaining to relationships. How many of us still hold fast to the original formula for life given to man by Yah? What society only passes laws that have undergone the litmus test of being in harmony with Yah?

Which ones among us have determined that every aspect of any relationship we are a part of must meet the criteria established by Yah? The answers to each of these questions will in most instances be in the negative. This automatically means that whatever you are attempting to do is destined to fail. If you don't follow the formula for life given to you by your creator, how can you avoid the resulting problems? It would take a simple minded moron, to buy a new car, disregard the car's creator's instructions in the owner's manual and still expect problem free driving.

If the manual directs you to use unleaded gas, would you use water? If it said to use 40 weight motor oil, would you use body lotion? If the car's head lights required 30 amp fuses, who would use 5 amps? Who would be foolish enough to subject their brand new car to this kind of abuse in the first place? Only a complete moron would expect good performance, after such abuse. I'm pretty sure that you would probably agree, that anyone that stupid, more than likely wouldn't own a new car anyway.

Yet, despite this obviously flawed and contradictory thinking, an entire world has disregarded their creator's owner's manual for maintaining life. Then, just like our moron friend, they still expect good performance out of life! We live in societies that not only pass laws to endorse activities that are contrary to Yah, but they even pass laws that outlaw Yah!!! In America for instance, it is illegal to pray to or teach about Yah in schools. Is it any wonder that the students have become immoral, undisciplined and demonic? Yet many people still wonder why the children use drugs, kill one another and generally display such abhorrent behavior!!!

Earlier in this book, we discussed the fact, that the lack of discernment was the single most detrimental factor in our lives. It is the lack of discernment that prevents everyone from seeing these great contradictions and implementing corrective measures. Most of the things that spell disaster for us, are built into how we perceive things. This lack of discernment mars our perceptions. We therefore suffer from a warped perspective of reality, causing us to follow improper courses of action and erroneously expect a proper outcome.

The same imbalance exists with most personal and marital relationships. The "mating ritual" in most "modern or worldly societies" usually follows this or a similar pattern. Two people will meet in a bar, at a party, at work, at school, at church or in some other social situation. They will begin dating, go out a few times and then start to have sex (sometimes the sex starts earlier, but rarely much later than the third or fourth date). If they enjoy the sex, they will feel that they are "in love" and maybe they will move into a house or apartment together. One day they decide to get married.

Rarely, in these situations, is there any, or more rarely the correct consciousness about whether or not the way they are proceeding is rooted in Yah. If this is a version of how your relationship was formed and developed, it is perfectly understandable that you are experiencing marital difficulties.

If the development of your relationship did not follow this pattern exactly, but was still not developed in accordance with the principles, standards and procedures enunciated under the "Perfect Paradigm," you will likewise experience marital problems that will require work to resolve.

It is important to remember that we are actually talking about relationships that are the product of two different worlds. There is on the one hand, the re-emerging world of Yah. Yah's world is establishing the criteria for a New World Order and is the progenitor of Divine Marriage, as a system. As such, the problems encountered in these marriages are not due to flaws in the marital system itself. These problems are instead concommitant to the people and their inability to shake off worldly concepts concerning relationships and embrace those which are Holy.

On the other hand, there is the decaying "modern world." This world represents the old paradigm and its marital systems ie., monogamy, polygyny, etc. These systems are the primary source, from which all of the problems originate. The marriages under these systems, therefore experience problems caused by the flawed systems themselves as well as the people's attempts to try and make these unrighteous systems work.

Since it is the systems which create the problems and cause them to fester, it is therefore these systems which require changing before the problems they produce can be resolved.
The "modern world" offers no real solutions to the problems encountered in today's marriages. Any serious attempt at real resolutions would require the total dismantling of these societies, (which we know they are not prepared to do).

We therefore understand that we can only inject the corrective principles of Yah into marriages where the individuals are willing to make correct choices independently. You will have to change from worldly concepts of marriage to the Yah inspired Kingdom concept of Divine Marriage. It will be necessary to begin to think and act in a new way, if you are to correct the discrepencies that exist in your marriage.

You must be willing to put the improper things you have been taught behind you and accept a new paradigm based on the truth of Yah. This world has moved away from Yah in all things and has rejected Yah and His order. As stated earlier, the Preferred Order of Yah is the only formula that can correct a relationship that has gone awry. The Preferred Order is Yah, man, woman, children.

Men, you must stop and place your hand in Yah's hand, and begin to reorder your life and those of your wife/wives and children according to His plan and guidelines. Women, you must stop and place your hand in the hand of your Yah-directed man, and follow and assist him in maintaining the family on the path of Yah. This will place you both in a corrective cycle that will lead to a proper understanding, a reconfigured Divine Relationship and a Divine Marraige.

"And he spoke a parable unto them saying: No man putteth a piece of a new garment upon an old; if so then both the new maketh a tear and the piece that was taken out of the new agreeth not with the old. And no man putteth new wine into old wineskins; else the new wine will burst the wineskins, and be spilled, and the wineskins will perish."

Luke 6:36-37

The Difficulties With People

This section is going to address some issues which might offend some men or women. That however, is not the objective of this section. Its purpose is to cause each of us to take another look at how we are handling ourselves in our relationships. If we are guilty of some of the behavior discussed, so be it, **change**. If you are not guilty of them but your spouse is, use this guide to help them change.

We are all guilty to some extent and we must admit this if we are to go beyond the lie. Whatever the case, don't merely be offended, instead be shocked by your conduct, shocked into making the change required to strengthen your marriage.

In the minds of all people there is a thought or impulse that makes them feel the need to be right. I don't mean to imply by this, that all people are striving to achieve correctness. There is a major difference between being right, as it relates to that mental impulse and striving to be correct. The mental and often emotional impulse to be right is motivated by a desire to attain a position of hegemony in a given situation and has nothing to do with seeking correctness.

In many instances people are simply playing the age old game of "one upsmanship." It is a terrible misnomer to refer to it as a "game" because there is absolutely nothing about it that can even remotely be considered fun or playful. In an effort to always appear right, people are given to say things or do things in a manner that will ensure, to the greatest degree possible, that their wants or desires are gratified. In an effort to achieve the "up position," some are prepared to outright lie, or to assuage a non-compliant conscience, merely to misrepresent the truth by simply leaving out relevant facts.

"One upsmanship" is a self protective mechanism developed in a social structure that is bent on exploiting everyone and everything to the maximum degree possible. In this structure, you are either the predator or the prey, with the former being the preferred position. Appearing right helps to place you and keep you in the "up position." This is generally the desired objective behind the impulse to be right.

Striving for correctness, on the other hand, is recognizing that the only way to achieving the worthwhile things in life is to move continuously closer to Yah. That observing the laws of truth, justice, love, mercy and peace is the thing that matters and that it will bring joy to our lives.

In many, if not most marriages in today's world, it is the appearance of right as opposed to striving for correctness that is the norm. The minds of the parties in these marriages are too often preoccupied with thoughts of winning out over their partner and not of their joint success in the marriage. It often becomes a situation where their efforts to get what they want from the marriage forms the obstacles which block them from what they want to obtain.

People have a tendency to act as though they are doing something that they really are not or say things that are not true in as convincing a manner as possible, then believe that this will entitle them to the rewards that can only come from the truth. This manifest itself in one form with men and another form with women. There are also historical untruths on which we have built our relationships that must be reconciled before we can find the truly sustainable, harmonious relationships we desire.

Unfortunately, people have been living these lies and misinterpretations for so long that the real truth is hardly even recognizable any more even when presented with irrefutable proof. I am presenting to you the absolute truth in all that is discussed in this book. My motive remains to reach your inner mind and spirit where only truth dwells and pray that you will allow yourself to acknowledge what you know in your heart is correct.

The Difficulties With Men

Men are completely hopeless prior to committing to seeking oneness with Yah. It is only after this commitment, that they evolve up to the point of being merely difficult. The blessing however, of a man committed to Yah is that, even though things in life may still be difficult at times, it's only because he is yet on his way to Yah and not because he is still moving away. The problems presented by those thusly committed are akin to growing pains and are to be expected and not dreaded. As he matures in Yah, these disorders will dissipate like so many
adolescent facial pimples.

The serious concern is not so much the difficulties but whether or not he will continue on the committed path. The necessary changes will only take place in those who are committed and remain on the path on which Yah has placed them. So don't get too worked up over what appear to be problems. Both the man and the woman need to remember, that he is in lordship training and Son of Yah training at the same time. For a man who is a member of the Hebrew Community this is a normal part of life but for one who is a product of today's world, this can seem a daunting challenge.

Men tend to view life from a perspective that is black and white, plain and simple. Once committed to a course, they will usually follow through and go all the way. This does not mean that they won't make mistakes or have periods of regression or even have areas which represent hurdles over which they have great difficulty climbing. This sometimes translates into stone walls and inflexibility in their marriages.

At times some men may seem too hard core or dogmatic to live with harmoniously. But as I said, "most men tend not to vacillate, they either do it or they don't." The difficulty sometimes comes with trying to find the proper balance. It is better in most cases however, to err on the side of over zealousness when it comes to points of order and law than to fall short of the mark with too much permissiveness.

If your marriage seems to be "all strained up" because of what is considered an unacceptable excess of over zealousness, it is time to call in the priest for more clarity on the laws. This will help everyone gain a better perspective. In most marriages where there are problems stemming from the husband imposing "too much law," that is usually not the case. The problem in most of these instances is usually that the man is too rigid and cannot strike the proper balance between what his responsibilities are and what to expect the law to deliver.

The hardliners sometimes think that they can be aloof or detached and that law will force their wives to love and appreciate them. Their tendencies are to order their wives around as though their relationship needed nothing other than legality to exist. Often these men are guilty of being insensitive, generally not out of a desire to cause distress but out of a need for direction and guidance. Many times these men think they are doing things in the manner that they should be done. Even when their wives voice their concerns, these men feel their complaints are unfounded and self-serving. At this point, because he cannot see himself, it is time to get help from the priest or other competent sources.

Sometimes a man will feel that because he can have more than one wife, he needn't try to resolve issues with his wives. He may think, if he does not feel like being bothered with the issues pertaining to one, that he can simply spend his time with another. This is of course his prerogative, but as lord, it is his responsibility to foster harmony in his entire household. He is therefore obligated to resolve issues in order to make life for his entire family harmonious. He cannot play one wife against another or disregard one wife in favor of another.

A lord is master of his home but he is not allowed to intimidate his wives or create a situation wherein they cannot hold discussions with him regarding their concerns. The wives must at all times, remain respectful, but they cannot be shut off from voicing their observations and feelings about legitimate issues. There are occasions when men need to be more honest and forthcoming.

A good example of this is when a man begins to develop interests in another woman. Some men will not be prepared to tell their wives the truth about what they are involved in. Coming from monogamous backgrounds, their first tendency is to lie or be ambiguous about the women in whom they may be interested. Though these men are in transition from one cultural paradigm to another and the difficulties they face are understandable, they cannot allow these difficulties to undermine their integrity.

The husband has the responsibility to determine the point at which he should talk to his wife concerning another woman in whom he might be interested. It is wise however, to do this as soon as possible after his decision to allow the relationship to develop. This allows everyone to begin the transition simultaneously. Of course, there are some wives who don't make it easy for their husband to come home and talk about these things.

This however, does not excuse a husband from proceeding with his responsibility to handle things in the proper manner. He cannot allow his fear of how his wife will probably react, to cause him to "wimp out." He should realize that avoiding telling her will not lessen or otherwise alter her reaction to the news anyway.

Men must acknowledge at some point that they have created the situation where division has come between the man and the woman and first correct the historical wrongs and then their personal wrongs. This does not alter the need for the woman to correct her behavior but even with these corrections in place, the relationship cannot be mended until man first puts things between him and the woman straight. To straighten things out we men must take a historical journey and be prepared to undergo a spiritual catharasis that can only be performed by facing the truth about what we have been and what we have done to women.

In the garden , Yah gave man dominion over all things in the creation including woman. At that time there was no division between the two. Man was then and remains even now, the one that was given dominion by Yah and is therefore responsible for the outcome. Woman was made as a helpmate fit for man and her estrangement from man was not her doing.
It was his fault.

He was a willing participant and more than that, close examination of the biblical record shows he actually put her up to getting the forbidden fruit for both of them. Adam wimped out when Yah questioned him in the garden concerning his knowledge of nakedness and his transgressing the commandment to not eat of the tree. He sold her down the river by turning "state's evidence" and placing the blame on her in an effort to save himself.

This early display of man's cowardice was designed to cause the woman to take the fall by herself. He even tried to lay the blame on Yah for providing him with a helpmate. This is the first recorded case of wife abuse in the historical account of man's relationship with woman.

"And He said , who told thee that thou wast naked? Hast thou eaten of the tree, whereof I commanded thee that thou shouldest not eat? And the man said, **the woman** *whom* **thou gavest to be with me,** *she gave me of the tree and I did eat."* (emphasis, the author's)

Genesis 3:10-12

But since that moment in our history, man has continued to misuse, abuse, lie to and in general, take advantage of the woman Yah gave him. Right now, today, men still lie to their women about where they're going, where they've been, what they're doing and above all, with whom. She has been exploited to the point where she has difficulty finding any dignity in being the woman Yah created her to be. The woman Yah gave to us has been reduced to a commodity that is bartered for by the misguided fallen man.

Meanwhile, this woman has remained at man's side through thick and thin, not without issues (which is understandable given her abuse by man) but remained there none-the-less. Men must acknowledge this wrongful behavior toward women and change their ways. In addition to the types of difficulties we've discussed here, men, including many of those who are in the process of returning to Yah, also contribute to marital problems by reacting improperly to problems created by women that have been corrupted by men.

Difficulties With Women

Ultimately, we must all understand that the main source from which most marital problems spring is the breakdown of order. Either the man, the woman or both are functioning in opposition to their mandate from Yah. In either case, their personal conduct reflects this disobedience and the results are marital problems. Submission to Yah's laws is the only way to avoid having these problems.

Men who are in the process of returning to Yah, have demonstrated a remarkable proclivity toward becoming lawful and submitting to His will. However, there is still a great deal of work to be done by them, as I have just pointed out. Women likewise have done a creditable job in this regard, but as a whole, they continue to lag somewhat behind their male counterparts in some areas. An illustration of this became graphically clear recently during an informal gathering, of some men and women from the Hebrew Community of which I was a part.

The question came up in the discussion concerning fairness in determining what teachings were needed by whom. One of the women commented that it appeared as if women were unfairly singled out more often than men to receive teachings regarding submission and humility. She went on to say that men were required to submit in almost as many situations as were women. Men, she said, had to submit to community leadership, to Yah, to the laws which govern them, to community rules and regulations and even to women in some circumstances. So why was there so much more emphasis placed on teaching women about humility and submission than is placed on teaching men?

It certainly was a valid question and caused a lively dialog to ensue. At a certain point, I turned to our International Ambassador who was also a part of the group and asked him how long he and I had been friends and how long I had served under his leadership?

He thought for a minute and said, "About twenty years." I asked him would he explain to everyone how closely we worked together and how regularly we saw each other? Again he thought for a few minutes then said, "We always worked very closely and for many years you served as my chief-of-staff and we saw one another daily."

By this time everyone was wondering what was the purpose of this line of questions because it didn't seem to be germane to the issues on the floor. Then I asked if in all those years, after all the time we spent together and all the situations we faced, did he remember a time when I had raised my voice to him? He immediately answered "not one time." I then asked was there ever a time that I disrespected him or stormed out of a room slamming a door or even used arrogant body language when addressing him?

When he answered this time he stated that not only had I never done any of those things in the twenty years of our relationship but that there had never been a time that I told him "no" when he requested something of me. I then asked other men in the room about their relationships with others in leadership and received similar answers. When I finished with them, I asked the married women if they had ever raised their voices or acted disrespectful to their husbands during their years of marriage. They all answered "Yes".

When asked how often, their responses were that they couldn't count the times. They each admitted that they still sometimes slipped in that regard. The questions went on to explore the relationships between women and other females who were in leadership. We discovered that while these women had made monumental strides compared to women in the rest of the world, they were still in much greater need of submission and humility teachings than their male counterparts. This completely impromptu mini-study showed us that the females needed to learn more about how to submit if they are to become the women Yah intended them to be.

It follows that since failure to submit is the central cause of marital problems, submitting to the will of Yah will turn things around. This cannot be accomplished unless we are prepared to acknowledge who and what is causing the breakdown. It is clear that men do contribute to the problem and in some cases are the total problem. We also have to accept that, as the lord, it is the man who must assume ultimate responsibility for the success or failure of the marriage. However, we must also accept that women do create many problematic situations.

Most women will submit to the will of Yah — **"conditionally."** Many don't see or understand that they can only follow and submit to Yah by following and submitting to the Son of Yah. Among those who do understand this, many feel that it is a conditional arrangement which they can alter according to how they see things. These women feel that they have the right to pick and choose the time, places and issues to which they should submit.

If she agrees with where he is going; she will let him lead her there, if not, she will chart her own course. If she wants him to do what he is attempting to do; she will allow him to do it, if not, she will plague him or constantly nag him until he abandons his objective. If his words are her words or his thoughts are her thoughts; she will encourage them and work to fulfill them, if not, she will condemn them and rebel.

This Is Not The Manner In Which To Fulfill The Will Of Yah. This Is Fulfilling The Will Of The Woman, Under The Guise Of Fulfilling The Will Of Yah!!!

Submission to Yah must be a total and unconditional commitment; anything else is unacceptable. For even a professed anarchist will go along with those things with which he agrees. It is this **"conditional submission,"** on the part of some women, that is at the base of our most serious marital problems. I want to give you a scenario with which most are familiar.

On a typical evening a man comes home from work and finds his wife in a foul mood. She's barely talking and what little she is saying is being said in monosyllables. Her mouth is stuck out and her face is contorted into a perpetual scowl. She is storming through the house, slamming doors, being impatient with the children and making anyone, unlucky enough to cross her path, miserable. The air is literally thick with the negative energy exuding from her every pore.

The husband will ask what's the matter and she will answer in a very strained, harsh or snappish voice, "Nothing." He may ask her several times what is the matter and she will continue with the lie that there is nothing out of order. By which time she will probably be accusing him of badgering her and being inconsiderate. It's obvious that there is a problem but she exacerbates matters by not humbly explaining what it is so that it can be resolved. Her failure to honor his questions with truthful answers eventually angers him and the situation escalates to "Def-Con 4".

In time, a full fledged blowout occurs, causing all kinds of residual flare ups which can sometimes last for weeks or longer. The husband finds himself wondering, how did all this get started and what to do about it? He never found out what the original problem was and probably never will. Suffice it to say, all of this could have been avoided if the wife had chosen submission and humility as opposed to displaying her displeasure in this manner.

There are sometimes periods in the lives of people when no appreciable problems exist. For reasons known only to herself, a woman will think of something negative. She will then analyze the thought and determine within her mind that the thought is correct. At this point, she will begin to conduct herself as though this is reality. It has nothing to do with whether or not this is in fact real. The mere fact that she believes it is real, is all that she requires to establish it as a fact and a reality.

If her thought is that her lord has been deceitful or unfaithful or did anything out of order, she will begin to treat him as though he was guilty of her imagined infraction. In other words, she will become the prosecutor, judge and jury in a case against her lord which she fabricated in her mind. She will accuse him, try him, convict him, sentence him and if she could, she would have him thrown into prison without a hearing. His only saving grace, in these situations, is the fact that generally she doesn't have the power to implement her judgements.

Humility and unconditional submission to Yah's will, would never permit a wife to conduct herself in such a manner. She would respect her lord and would therefore, not disregard his questions nor answer them untruthfully. She would likewise never falsely accuse him nor doubt him without just cause. (Her belief does not constitute "just cause"). Naturally, these reality defying scenarios, which many women are predisposed to create, are not pleasing to their lords and often incur their wrath and unpleasant repercussions.

The regularity of these imagined offences and subsequent trauma, places a major strain on even the best relationships. She becomes her own worst enemy and undermines her own efforts to attain the love, happiness and joy she seeks. Examine this old parable about the sun and the wind to see an example of how women often defeat their own purposes.

189

One day the sun and the wind were discussing who was the strongest. Each argued very convincingly why he felt his strength was greater than that of the other. Finally, it was decided that they needed to have a contest to settle the dispute. At the same time, there was a man walking along the beach wearing a cloak. The wind pointed to the man and said, "Because I'm stronger, I bet I can get that man's cloak off and you can't." To which the sun replied, "I accept this challenge because it is I who have the greatest strength."

To accomplish his objective, the wind began to blow with all his strength and power. The more the wind blew the colder it became and the tighter the man held onto his cloak. The wind blew and blew and blew, all to no avail. In time, the wind became so exhausted that he was forced to give up and admit that he could not get the cloak off the man.

It was now the sun's turn to try and the wind said, "Surely if I could not get that cloak off with all my strength you don't stand a chance." The sun then began to shine. Soon it began to get warmer and warmer, until it became very hot on the beach. At this point, the man who had loosened his cloak when it began to warm up, took his cloak completely off and carried it over his arm.

There is a law that instructs us to try and get warm when the temperature is cold and seek to cool off when it gets hot. The wind was attempting to force a situation in violation of this law and failed. The sun, on the other hand, moved in harmony with the law and was successful.

All too often women will conduct themselves like the wind when seeking to secure themselves in a marital relationship. They will ignore the laws which govern them and will try to force their lords into doing what they feel he should be doing.

190

The love or sensitivity they desire is not encouraged by their behavior. Instead, it is removed further from them as a result of their behavior.

A woman will raise hell with her man and then wonder why he doesn't feel like kissing or hugging her an hour later. There are ways to deal with situations that won't exacerbate the original problem that a woman perceives. But they require that the woman approach the issue with a degree of humility that is lacking in most modern liberated women.

The woman who violates Yah's laws by standing "toe-to-toe" with her lord will never accomplish her objective but will only cause greater and greater estrangement, regardless of its origins, just like the wind.

Resolving The Difficulties

There is no end to the problems affecting the marriages of today. We can discusss them from here to eternity if we are so inclined and will always find one more lurking in an obscure corner of the relationship. We can talk about solutions for just as long and not improve a single marriage. There are a thousand books on the subject, written by single or divorced people who are offering you help with your situation that they could not effectively employ in their own. They may be sincere and really want to help but only Yah can help and they are not offering His help.

There are many writers that offer various religious perspectives on what to do and how to do it. Unfortunately, since their understanding of Yah is at best confused and at worst deliberately contrary, their solutions are unworkable. It was their understanding or at least their professed understanding that created the mess from which we're trying to extricate ourselves at this point. Surely they can't be taken seriously when they come forth offering solutions to problems they have created.

There are psychiatrists, psychoanalysts, and marriage counselors galore, all putting forth their positions on how to correct marriages gone wrong. We read Ann Landers and Dear Abby, we watch Oprah Winfrey, Phil Donoghue, Jerry Springer, Montel Williams and a host of others all vying for our attention and discipleship, as they attempt to show us the way to better lives and interpersonal relationships. They all get their direction from the same source, therefore, their road maps all have the same errors. Forget the fancy "motivational seminars" and "sensitivity sessions." These things have not worked, cannot work and will not work at some later date.

There are things you should do and things you should not do that are regulated by the laws of Yah. Understand, acknowledge and follow them for the permanent solutions, to not only marital problems, but to all problems. In the Kingdom of Yah at Jerusalem, this is relatively easy to do because we stand on the foundation of Yah. This means that we do everything in accordance with His plan, and handle problems according to His conflict resolution process.

When a Divine Marriage exists and the spouses are in complete agreement that they are governed by Yah, the only question that can ever come up regarding a solution to a problem is "What would Yah have us to do concerning this issue?" This means that there can never be a personal conflict between a man and his wife. Conflict can only exist, between a position held on an issue and a law or guideline of Yah. Therefore, anyone holding such a position does not have a conflict with their spouse but instead, has a controversy with Yah and must change their position on the issue.

This is clearly illustrated in the following scenario. A husband wants to have a dog in the house as a pet because when he was growing up, his family always had a dog in the house. His wife, on the other hand, did not want a dog in the house because they never had dogs in her house as she was growing up. They could argue and fight over the issue and whoever had the most might would probably win and their will would carry the day.

Another possibility is that one could simply yield to the other for peace's sake or love's sake or the dog's sake, any of which could end the confrontation but not necessarily solve the problem. The Kingdom solution would be to inquire of the priesthood or other competent sources regarding the law or guidelines governing dogs as pets.

Whichever spouse was not in harmony with the answer would simply adjust their position to that of the Kingdom guideline. In the Kingdom things are no longer based on might but are instead, based on what's truly right. There are still problems to be worked out but we now have the proper paradigm from which to work.

Everyone can be a part of a Divine Marriage; it is the way Yah planned for all of His children. You must return to Yah to experience the process that works. This is the truth, plain and simple. Come to Dimona, Israel and see the everlasting results.

"Then shall ye return, and discern between the righteous and the wicked, between him that serveth (Yah) and him that serveth him not."

Malachi 3:18

The Truth will appear to be your enemy; the lie your friend. That causes people to prefer (in many instances, though they recognize the logic and practicality of the Truth) to cling to the acknowledged lie. In essence, you cannot have both worlds nor both ways. You can't meet God halfway; He demands total commitment. Now, in addition to learning this new truth, comes the responsibility of making some painful decisions. Don't compromise.

Remember, things never get better alienated from God. Whatever way the Master Deceiver (the devil) makes it appear, things are only getting worse. God, the Father of His creations, is not going to change your life for the worse. Eyes have not seen, neither have ears heard what God has in store for those that return unto Him.

**The Messiah And The End Of This World
by Ben Ammi, Communicators Press**

For additional copies of this book or online relationship and marriage counseling services contact Dr. Shaleahk at haraymiel@yahoo.com or visit our website www.withoutpretense.com

For more information on the Hebrew Community go to www.kingdomofyah.com

Glossary of New World Translations

Adultery – an act of sexual intercourse with the wife of another man; a married woman having sexual intercourse with a man other than her husband; a man who causes his wife to have sexual intercourse with a man other than himself; spiritually pursuing other gods.

Anointed, The - The Holy Personage of the one sanctified and appointed by Yah to return to His people and establish the prophetic Kingdom of Yah.

Daughter of Yah - (See regenerated woman)

Defacto/Pseudo Marriage - An unofficially declared marriage which is only similar to a legitimate marriage; one which takes on the form without the substance of a true marriage.

Discern - To detect with senses other than vision; to see or understand the difference; the ability to see and understand the difference between what is right and what is wrong; seeing with a spiritual eye opened by Yah due to one's humble submission to His will.

Discernment - The quality of being able to grasp and comprehend what is obscure or obvious; a power to see what is not evident to the average mind but only to those who pursue Yah.

Divine - That which is in a manner pleasing unto Yah; Yah has to be the thought that produces all substance, because everything is subject to His will.

Hebrew Israelite - One who has crossed over from the satanically influenced life of the world to the purity and holiness of life under Yah.

Holy - That which has been sanctified and set aside from the things of the world.

Humility - The state of being submissive to the will of Yah.

Inactive - During the time of a woman's menstrual cycle she is not to engage in certain activities such as, cooking, sleeping with her husband or having physical contact with him or others. Throughout this period she is considered "inactive."

Kepote - Crocheted or knitted head coverings worn by males.

Kingdom of Yah - A New World Order governed by men that are governed by Yah; a society set in order by men set in order by Yah; a home established by the Yah-family wherein children honor their father and mother, woman respects her man and man is in the image of Yah.

Law - The light and essence of what is required to set man on the path and show him the way back to Yah. The instructions and commandments of Yah. The guidelines of life for people living under the rule of Yah.

Lord - Ruler, master, great teacher, or the one you obey; a husband governed by Yah.

Lorship - The position or office of a lord.

Messianic - Relating to, marked by or advocating; believing in or carrying out those things mandated by the Messiah; being brought under the direct command of Yah in order to go forth as representatives of Yah's truth on earth.

Minister - Chief administrators within the governing structure of the Kingdom of Yah.

Monogamy - The custom or state of being married to one person at a time.

Monogyny - The practice or state of having only one wife at a time.

Naysayer - One who advocates or promotes negative positions on issues connotating a negative spirited individual i.e., one who is always disgruntled and can never agree.

New World Order - A new arrangement of lifestyle and purpose, being cycled back unto Yah and a life wherein His principles rule supreme; a divine society governed by men who are governed by Yah; a new social order of oneness with Yah and equality among men, with new values and holy standards of behavior.

Paradigm - An example; the parameter in which something exists or is viewed.

Polygamy - The state or practice of having more than one spouse at a time.

Polygyny - The state or practice of having more than one wife at a time.

Preferred Order of Yah - The hierarchy established by Yah for governing all things in the creation; the holy management structure for the human family which is Yah, man, woman and children.

Prince - The prophesied disciples who would govern with the Messiah upon his return; Holy Council Member within the governing structure of the Kingdom of Yah.

Practical Considerations- All the important and not so important things that make up your life, i.e., likes, dislikes, perspectives, habits, occupation, education, finances, etc.

Prophetic Priesthood - Order of Holy men spoken of in the scriptures, who would emerge as the teachers of the law and spiritual guides for the people; the holy administrators of spiritual affairs in the Kingdom of Yah.

Pursuer - One who seeks to attain harmony with the entity above them in the chain of command, represented by the Preferred Order of Yah i.e., man pursues Yah, woman pursues man and children pursue parents.

Regenerated Man - A man reborn, who submits to the New World Order way of life where truth and discipline are the essential prescriptions for spiritual growth and development.

Regenerated Woman - A woman reborn, who submits to the New World Order way of life where truth and discipline are the essential prescriptions for spiritual growth and development.

Saint - A citizen of the Kingdom of Yah; one who orders his life in accordance with the cycles of Yah.

Sin - Every work, action or deed that is not done for the glorification and sanctification of the true and living Yah of Israel.

Son of Yah - (See regenerated man)

Spirit of Err - Satanic, evil spirit or force which may possess a person or groups of people to be totally in opposition to Yah; the spirit/force behind all things wicked, perverse, deadly and unjust.

Yah - The Creator; the spiritual force representing righteousness, love, peace and all things positive and good.

Yah's Divine Cycles - The perpetual system of laws designed by Yah to keep the creation and its inhabitants in Divine Order and eternal harmony with His Holy Will.

Yeshua - The true Hebrew name for the Anointed Son of Yah who symbolized the word of Yah in the midst of the people; the biblical personage erroneously referred to by many as Jesus.

Bibliography

God the Black Man and Truth By Ben Ammi
Published by Communicators Press
Washington, D.C.

God and the Law of Relativity By Ben Ammi
Published by Communicators Press
Washington D.C.

The Messiah and the End of This World By Ben Ammi
Published by Communicators Press
Washington, D.C.

Fit For Life II By Harvey and Marilyn Diamond, M.D.
Published by Warner Books
New York, New York

New Scofield Reference Bible
Published by Oxford University Press
New York, New York

The World Almanac and Book Of Facts
Published by World Almanac Books
Mahwah, New Jersey

ISBN 141201722-X

9 781412 017220